"Then **Belichick** Said to **Brady**..."

The Best New England Patriots Stories Ever Told

Jim Donaldson

TRIUMPH
B O O K S

Library of Congress Cataloging-in-Publication Data

Donaldson, Jim.
    Then Belichick said to Brady— : the best New England Patriots stories ever told / Jim Donaldson.
        p. cm.
    Includes bibliographical references.
    ISBN-13: 978-1-60078-239-8
    ISBN-10: 1-60078-239-6
    1. New England Patriots (Football team)—History. I. Title.
    GV956.N36D67 2009
    796.332'640974461—dc22
                                                            2009025247

This book is available in quantity at special discounts for your group or organization. For further information, contact:

Triumph Books
542 South Dearborn Street
Suite 750
Chicago, Illinois 60605
(312) 939-3330
Fax (312) 663-3557
www.triumphbooks.com

Printed in U.S.A.
ISBN: 978-1-60078-239-8
Design by Patricia Frey
Photos courtesy of Getty Images except where otherwise indicated

To Sandra, who has written the best chapters of my life

table of
contents

foreword

I've known Jim Donaldson since 1982, the year I was drafted by the New England Patriots. Over my three-decade career as a Patriots player and employee, Jim has been a constant for me, first as a journalist and then as a friend. Having covered the New England Patriots since 1979, he is uniquely qualified to tell the story of the franchise.

When I gave my Pro Football Hall of Fame speech in August 2008, I made a point to speak about my high school motto, "Truth, Honor, and Light." Frank Verducci, my coach at Barringer High School in Newark, New Jersey, used this motto as a tool to teach his players the proper mind-set for the game of football. In *Truth*, we were taught to recognize our strengths as well as our weaknesses and to admit our mistakes. In *Honor*, we were taught to be proud of our name and to represent our family, our team, and our community. In *Light*, we were taught the importance of education and learning.

The Patriots are the only professional team for which I've ever played or been affiliated with, and I have carried those values I learned in high school with me throughout my career. They have allowed me to always consider my association with this franchise as a badge of honor. When we were the worst in the league and when we were the best in the league, when we were awful and when we were great, I have always been proud to be a New England Patriot.

I never wavered during the tough years, even when friends suggested that I should try to leave the organization. Playing for the Sullivan family, I watched as they did everything they could to keep the franchise alive. Despite the cards they were dealt, I was always treated with the utmost professionalism. In 1994 the Kraft family brought new perspective and fresh ideas. I was fortunate to witness this up close when Robert Kraft, in his first year as owner, hired me immediately after my retirement. We began to market the team more aggressively and change the fan experience. The Krafts not only held their players accountable, they held the fans accountable for their behavior. They changed the perception of what it meant to be associated with the Patriots. They promised a Super Bowl championship, and they have delivered three. I have been lucky enough to be around for it all.

With all the recent success, the highlight of my career is still the 1985 season, which is one of the many subjects explored in this book. We had gotten close in 1984, winning nine games and having Raymond Berry step in midway through the season. We had a renewed sense of what our potential was, and Berry was the perfect coach for the team at that time. The team made a pact that we would all participate in the off-season conditioning program, an experience that strengthened our bond as teammates. Five games into the 1985 season, though, we hadn't reached our full potential, and our chance to capitalize was slowly slipping away from us. Much has been made of my tirade in the locker room after the Cleveland Browns game, when my emotions and desire to win got the best of me. That game jump-started us, and we went on to have what was at that point the best and most exciting Patriots season in the franchise's history. We qualified for the playoffs as a wild card and went on to win the AFC championship by beating the Jets, Raiders, and Dolphins—winning all three games on the road—before losing to a tremendous Chicago Bears team in Super Bowl XX. It was a truly great year for the team, the fans, and the entire New England region.

As the years have slipped by, the memories of that season and many others have become ancient history. But those who were around to witness them can still relay the stories in vivid detail. That is where Jim Donaldson comes in.

Andre Tippett
New England Patriots Hall of Fame, 1999
Pro Football Hall of Fame, 2008

acknowledgments

John Hannah says, in the pages of this book, "The greatest time in my life was being in that locker room. I've never been able to find anything to replace it. I wish I could do it all over again. I'd do it in a heartbeat."

I could say much the same thing about my life in the press box.

I never wanted to do anything else other than write about sports, and I've never regretted the decision. It's been a great time. I wish I could do it all over again. I'd do it in a heartbeat.

The 2010 season will mark the beginning of the fifth decade in which I've covered the New England Patriots. My first season was 1979, so 2009 will be the 31st year I've been writing about the team. I've seen some unforgettable games in that time, but it's the people I've met over the years that I'll always remember because they've given me my fondest memories.

Many of those people helped immeasurably in the recalling and retelling of these Patriots stories. People like Ron Hobson, who covered the Patriots from their first season in 1960 until his retirement after the 2007 season and who is responsible for turning me from a pretty good tennis player into a not-very-good golfer; longtime Patriots play-by-play man Gil Santos, who tells these Patriots stories in a basso profundo voice made for radio; Gino Cappelletti, who as star player, then assistant coach, and now as analyst for nearly 30 years on the radio broadcast of the team's games truly has seen it all—from the team's first training camp through its five Super Bowl appearances.

A tip of the Patriots cap to coaches Raymond Berry, Bill Parcells, Ron Erhardt, Ron Meyer, and Pete Carroll—all of whom were a joy to cover and to be around. To Joe Mendes, a great friend. And, sadly, to the late Bucko Kilroy, Dick Steinberg, and Bill McPeak, who took the time to teach me about the game they knew so much about. Thanks, also, to players such as Hannah, Steve Grogan, Pete Brock, Tom Brady, Tedy Bruschi, Andre Tippett, Jon Morris, Irving Fryar, Steve Nelson, Bob "Harpo" Gladieux, Troy Brown, and so many others who have made the Patriots so interesting, entertaining, and enjoyable over so many years.

xii   "Then Belichick Said to Brady..."

Most helpful in putting this book together were Bryan Morry, executive director of the Hall at Patriot Place; Casey O'Connell, always ready with quick answers to arcane questions; and O'Connell's boss in the Patriots media-relations department, team vice president Stacey James.

Nor could it have been finished without Meghan Donaldson, who since has taken her editing skills "across the pond" to a publishing house in Dublin; Lynda and Al Bagley, whose contributions have been many and varied; and the supportive—and patient—Adam Motin at Triumph Books.

introduction

To measure how far the Patriots have come, you have to remember where they started.

They are the Johnny-come-latelies of Boston's major professional sports teams. When the Pats played their first season in 1960, the Red Sox had been in business since 1903 and had been playing in Fenway Park, their lyric little bandbox of a ballpark, beloved throughout New England, since 1912. The Red Sox hadn't won a World Series since 1918, but hope springs eternal—especially in the spring, when baseball season begins. And the Yankees couldn't win every year, could they? After all, the White Sox had won the American League pennant in 1959, using a combination of pitching, speed, and defense. And if they could knock off the powerful Yankees, then perhaps the Red Sox could, too—even though they didn't have much pitching, or any speed, or, for that matter, particularly good defense.

Still, the Red Sox were the team everybody in New England loved—even more than the Celtics, who were churning out championships as if on an assembly line—one after another, after another, after yet another.

In the fall of 1960 the Celts were on their way to what would be the third of a record eight straight NBA titles, part of an incredibly dominant string of nine championships in 10 years, and 11 in 13, from 1957 through 1969. Now that, sports fans, was a dynasty.

Then you had the Bruins. The beloved *B*s. One of the Original Six, who, in those days, were the Only Six. Hockey was strictly a regional game then, followed with fanaticism by its devotees in Montreal and Toronto, Chicago and Detroit, New York, and, you'd better believe, in Boston, the hub of hockey. Although the Bruins were nowhere near as good as the Celtics, it was harder to get a ticket for a hockey game than a basketball game at the Boston Garden.

It would have been perfectly understandable for Billy Sullivan's fledgling football franchise to be a distant fourth in fan appeal. Except they weren't even that. They were fifth, behind the New York Football Giants. The Giants were New England's football team then. Their games were telecast every Sunday throughout the region, and they were a treat to watch. They were the best team in the NFL's Eastern Division and featured the likes of Frank Gifford, Charlie Conerly, Sam Huff, Roosevelt Brown, Kyle Rote, Roosevelt Grier, Andy Robustelli—an array of stars.

So it was an uphill battle from the beginning for the Patriots. It was nice when they played for the AFL championship in 1963, but it wasn't a big deal, especially after they were trounced 51–10 by the Chargers in San Diego. People took notice when, after years of mediocrity (or worse), the Patriots went from 3–11 in 1975 to 11–3 in 1976. But they missed the playoffs the following year, and Chuck Fairbanks bolted for the University of Colorado the year after that, and so it wasn't until 1985, when the Patriots went to their first Super Bowl, that the team began to claim a truly meaningful share of the attention, and affection, of New England sports fans.

The arrival of Bill Parcells in 1993 put the Patriots front and center and, once Bill Belichick started winning championships, the Pats, once scorned and derided, were embraced, beloved, and cheered. They weren't merely popular, they suddenly, finally, were wildly popular. Where once they were hard-pressed to attract even 25,000 fans to games in Foxboro, the new Gillette Stadium was filled for every game.

It would be impossible in traditional old New England to supplant the Sox as No. 1 in the region. But it was, indeed, possible that the Patriots had become 1-A, far ahead of the Bruins and the Celtics too—even after the Celts snapped a long string of futility by winning their 17th championship in 2008.

Once a league laughingstock, the Patriots, under the ownership of Robert Kraft, had become a model franchise. Once largely ignored, the Pats now are widely imitated. Once a team that even New England sports fans cared little about, they now are a team that arouses emotions—both love and hate—across the country.

chapter 1

The Snow Game

Snow was falling.

No, that's not exactly right.

To say that snow was falling brings to mind a quiet, Currier and Ives scene of an idyllic New England winter evening.

It was anything but quiet at Foxboro Stadium the night of January 19, 2002.

Snow was swirling and whirling. The chilled fans in the sellout crowd of 60,292 were stamping their feet trying to keep warm and to spur on the Patriots, who were battling the Oakland Raiders in an AFC playoff game that would change the history of the franchise.

"It was a lot of snow," quarterback Tom Brady recalled, "and it started about three or four hours before the game."

The snow was pelting down heavily throughout the game—large, powdery flakes like feathers from a pillow that had burst open. The snow was blowing up, down, sideways, in any and all directions, making it seem as if the game was being played inside a giant snow globe. It was a winter wonderland. And, for Patriots fans, a football fantasyland.

Right there in the middle of it all was Adam Vinatieri, the Patriots' kicker. He was in the eye of the storm, and all eyes in Foxboro Stadium were on him.

There were 27 seconds remaining in the AFC semifinal playoff game, and the Patriots were trailing the Raiders 13–10. The ball was on the Oakland 28-yard line. Seven yards behind that, and 45 yards from the goal posts, was Vinatieri, standing in ankle-deep snow.

Adam Vinatieri kicks a 45-yard field goal to tie the game with 27 seconds left in the fourth quarter against the Oakland Raiders in the AFC Divisional Playoff Game on January 19, 2002. Photo courtesy of AP Images.

"There were three or four inches of snow on the ground," he said. "Whenever you get a few inches on the ground, and it's still falling, that makes it pretty tough. It was sticking to the bottom of your shoes, so you never really felt you could get sure footing. And we were out of timeouts, so we didn't have a chance to clear away the snow from the spot where we wanted to kick."

The fact that the Patriots even had a chance to kick and tie the game was a minor miracle. They trailed 13–3 after three quarters. But with Brady completing nine consecutive passes on his way to setting club playoff records for passing attempts (52), completions (32), and passing yards (312), the Pats cut their deficit to 13–10 with 7:52 left in the game when Brady capped a 67-yard drive by scrambling six yards for what would be his team's only touchdown.

The Raiders had a chance to wrap up the game when, with 2:24 remaining, they had a third-and-1 at their own 44. They gave the ball to Zack Crockett, who was stopped shy of the first down by linebacker Tedy Bruschi.

Oakland coach Jon Gruden wisely decided to punt. Troy Brown fielded the kick at the New England 19 and returned it 27 yards but fumbled when he was hit. Fortunately for the Patriots, their Pro Bowl special-teams specialist Larry Izzo recovered.

Brady threw for seven yards to running back Kevin Faulk just before the two-minute warning, after which he ran five yards himself for a first down at the Oakland 42 with 1:50 left in the game.

Then came the play for which the game always will be remembered— fondly in New England, frustratingly in Oakland. "The Tuck Rule Play will forever be a part of NFL legend," said Mike Pereira, the league's vice president of officiating. "Since the current system of instant replay was adopted, no reviewed play has been more debated or discussed."

Charles Woodson, the Raiders' All-Pro cornerback, came on a blitz, hitting Brady and knocking the ball loose as his arm was moving forward in either an attempt to pass the ball or as he was trying to bring it down and tuck it away.

Brad Sham, announcing the game nationally on radio, said, "Shotgun for Brady. Blitz. Back to throw. Rushed. Hit! Fumbled the football! It's still on the floor and the Raiders have recovered! This one's going to lead to the end of the season for the New England Patriots." That's how it looked to just about everyone watching, both in the snow-covered stands and on television.

It's certainly how Woodson saw it. "He pumped the ball, brought it back down," Woodson said. "Ball came out. Game over."

That was the way it seemed to Patriots safety Lawyer Milloy, standing on the sideline. "The game's over. That's what I was thinking," Milloy said. "The game is over." But it wasn't over. Far from it.

Because the play occurred in the last two minutes, there was a call for a review from Rex Stuart, the replay official in the press box. So Walt Coleman, the referee, went to the sideline and ducked under the hood of the replay monitor. While both teams waited tensely, he reviewed the play.

"I was hurting pretty bad," said Vinatieri, recalling his emotions. "And then, all of a sudden, they were reviewing it and giving us a ray of hope."

When Coleman finally emerged from under the replay hood, returned to the field, and turned on his microphone to announce his ruling, it was so quiet in the stadium you could hear a snowflake hit the ground.

"After reviewing the play," he said, "the quarterback's arm was going forward. It's an incomplete pass." The crowd roared. The Raiders groaned. The Patriots had a second life.

"From what I saw on the field," Coleman explained later, "I thought the ball came out before his arm was going forward, so that's why I ruled it a fumble. When I got over to the replay monitor and looked at it, it was obvious that his arm was coming forward. He was trying to tuck the ball, and they just knocked it out of his hand. His hand was coming forward, which made it an incomplete pass."

Brady, not surprisingly, agreed. Gruden, not surprisingly, did not.

"I knew I was throwing the ball," Brady said. "I'm glad they ruled it the way they did."

"I thought it was a fumble," Gruden said. "But the officials thought otherwise."

Patriots coach Bill Belichick insisted that the controversial ruling was the right one. "Anybody can complain about the rule all they want," he said, "but that's what it is. When you look at the play, that was the correct ruling."

What at first appeared to be a game-ending fumble was overturned on the basis of Rule 3, Section 21, Article 2 of the *NFL Rule Book*, which states, "When a player is holding a ball to pass it forward, any intentional forward movement of his arm starts a forward pass, even if the player loses possession of the ball as he is attempting to tuck it back toward his body. If the player has tucked the ball into his body and then loses possession, it is a fumble."

While the Patriots still had the ball, they still had to get into field-goal range. They did—barely—on the next play as Brady threw to wide receiver David Patten for 13 yards. They would have liked to get closer, but Brady's next two passes were incomplete and, after he gained a yard on third down, Vinatieri trotted carefully on to the field.

"When you're in a situation like that," he said, "it seems like everything slows down a little bit. You just have to focus and hope for the best.

"We were pushing the envelope a little bit. We wanted to get a little bit closer, obviously. That was a real low-percentage kick, especially in those conditions. How many times would I make it if you gave me a hundred shots? I don't know—10, maybe."

One in 10?

As far as Patriots fans are concerned, Vinatieri's kick was one in a million because it forever altered the history of a franchise that for most of its first four decades of existence was filled with far more frustration than glory.

"I was wearing the longest cleats I could get my hands on," he said. "They were like shark's teeth. When I went out there, I said to myself, 'Just kick it as best you can.' I tried to stay over my feet so I wouldn't slip. That's probably why the trajectory was so low."

That's one reason. Another was that he was kicking a ball that, in the freezing cold, was hard as a rock. Vinatieri also had to be careful with his approach in order to maintain his footing on the snowy ground. And who knew what would happen on the snap from Lonie Paxton or whether holder Ken Walter, who also was the Patriots' punter, could handle the ball properly?

"The job Kenny did was amazing," Vinatieri said. "He had to catch a ball with snow on one end and try to place it as quickly as he could."

The conditions were atrocious, but the snap was perfect. So was the hold.

And the kick? Aesthetically it wasn't much to look at. It was a low line drive that seemed to scuttle rather than soar toward the uprights.

But beauty truly is in the eye of the beholder, and when the ball went sailing through, it meant that kick would be remembered as a thing of beauty that would be a joy forever.

"I kind of line-drived it," Vinatieri said. "But, when I looked up, I knew it was going to be straight enough. I had to wait to see if it would be long enough. After that, it was time to be happy.

"Looking back at it, it's probably the most difficult field goal I've ever had to attempt. It's certainly the one I'm most proud of."

That's quite a statement from a kicker who would two times go on to boot last-second Super Bowl–winning field goals.

"We were down three points," he said. "I had to hit it to tie the game. And the field conditions—I don't know if I've ever kicked in conditions worse than that.

"I'll always remember the Super Bowl kicks. Those are great memories. But if you ask me what was my best kick ever, I'd have to say that one against Oakland."

That one kick—that one, magical, captured-in-a-snow-globe moment—marked a turning point for the Patriots, who only the year before had finished last in the AFC East at 5–11.

They won the coin toss to gain first possession in overtime and never gave up the ball. With Brady completing all eight of his pass attempts, the Patriots drove from their own 34 to the Oakland 5. Then with 6:31 showing on the scoreboard clock, Vinatieri kicked the game-winning 23-yard field goal. There was never a doubt he'd make that one. Not after he'd hit the one from 45.

"I felt like we had one taken away from us," said Jerry Rice, the Raiders' Hall of Fame wide receiver.

Twenty-five years earlier the Patriots felt they'd had a playoff victory taken away from them in Oakland. In that game referee Ben Dreith made a controversial roughing-the-passer call against Raymond "Sugar Bear" Hamilton.

The Raiders were trailing 21–17 and, with only 57 seconds left to play, were in a third-and-18 situation at the New England 27. Kenny "Snake" Stabler, Oakland's gutsy, gimpy-kneed quarterback, dropped back to pass and just managed to get the ball off—incomplete—when he was hit in the helmet by the flailing arm of nose tackle Hamilton.

Hamilton insisted he tipped the ball first, but all Dreith saw was the hit on Stabler. This came on the heels of a noncall when Oakland linebacker Phil Villapiano virtually tackled tight end Russ Francis on a third-down play that would have enabled the Patriots to maintain possession with the clock winding down. The whole situation left the Pats—and all of New England—with a bitter taste in their mouths.

It wasn't until nine years later, in 1985, that the Patriots would win their first NFL playoff game. They got to the Super Bowl that season, only to be trounced 46–10 by the Chicago Bears.

New England fans also were disappointed in their team's second trip to the Super Bowl, in the 1996 season, when the Patriots not only lost to the Packers, 35–21, but lost coach Bill Parcells to the New York Jets as well.

A dark cloud, it seemed, continued to hover over the franchise as it had from the beginning. That cloud hung until that snowy night of what would be the last game played in the old stadium in Foxboro. That magical night when Vinatieri's kick sailed through the snowflakes and the uprights, sending the Patriots on their way into a new era—one in which they'd win three Super Bowls in a span of just four years, go on to have a perfect 16–0 regular season in 2007, and become the dominant team of the decade.

"It was quite a way to send that stadium out," Brady said. "I mean, what more do you want from a football game?"

chapter 2

The Vagabonds

Their team name should have been the Vagabonds, not the Patriots. That's what they were: wanderers, moving from place to place with the changing seasons without a place of their own to call home.

They started out as the Boston Patriots and played their first three seasons at Boston University Field, off Commonwealth Avenue, on the site where baseball's Boston Braves played before moving to Milwaukee in 1953.

In 1963 the Patriots moved to Fenway Park, home of the Red Sox. They spent six seasons there before leaving to play at Boston College's Alumni Stadium in 1969, which almost burned down during a preseason game against the Redskins. In 1970, the year the Patriots moved again—this time to Harvard Stadium, where they weren't allowed to use the Ivy Leaguers' locker room and had to put on their uniforms in a nearby hotel and then walk across the university's playing fields to the stadium.

Through all those years, Billy Sullivan dreamed of building a stadium in Boston that his Patriots could call home. Unfortunately the dream was more of a nightmare.

The city had never been hospitable to professional football. Among the franchises that failed in Boston were the NFL Braves, who became the Redskins and moved in 1937 to Washington, and the Bulldogs of the American Football League. There also were the Shamrocks, who finished first in the AFL in 1936 but proved no luckier in the long run than any of Boston's other pro football teams, which also included the NFL Yankees (Is it any wonder they weren't popular in Beantown?) and the Bears, who played in the AFL in 1940.

But Sullivan felt the time was right to bring pro football back to Boston and began to seek an NFL franchise.

"My first memory of pro football," Sullivan's youngest son Patrick said, "is watching the championship game between the Giants and the Colts in 1958. After that game my father had his first 'serious' talk with me. I remember him saying to me, 'Patrick, this game is the game of the future.'"

Behind the scenes, Sullivan had been having conversations with the Red Sox, who were considering leaving antiquated Fenway Park—built in 1912—about sharing a domed stadium in the suburbs. With such a facility, Sullivan was confident that Bert Bell, the NFL commissioner, would grant Boston an expansion franchise.

The discussions reached the point where Sullivan had an elaborate scale model of the stadium constructed by an architectural firm. One of the primary backers of the proposed project, a brewing company in western Massachusetts, asked Sullivan to send the model to them for a look.

He was hesitant because the Red Sox were adamant about keeping the matter hush-hush. "But they paid for it, so we couldn't say no," Sullivan said of the beer executives. "We asked them to be very careful about publicity." They weren't.

A reporter from Springfield attended a cocktail party where the model was on display, and the story was all over the news the next day— April 1, 1958. Sullivan always remembered the date, because it was the same day he was named president of Metropolitan Oil Company.

"I was driving to work," he recalled, "and, on the radio, I heard a report about our stadium plans. The Red Sox were annoyed and walked away."

Soon after, Bell died. "I began to feel that I wasn't meant to have an NFL franchise," said Sullivan. Tenacity, however, was one of Sullivan's strong points.

As a longtime acquaintance once described him, "He's like sandpaper—he wears you down." In 1959 a new league with an old name—the American Football League—was taking shape. By that fall there were seven teams, and an eighth was needed.

There stood Sullivan, eager to get into the game—even in Boston, where most football fans could not have cared less. Most of them rooted for the Giants, who were one of the NFL's best teams and whose games were televised throughout New England every Sunday afternoon. With Boston College, Harvard, and other colleges playing on Saturdays, the Patriots decided that Friday nights would be best for them.

"We knew we had to go a long way to win over the fans," said Gino Cappelletti, one of the Patriots' first stars. Cappelletti later became an assistant coach and for many years has been the color commentator on the team's radio broadcasts. "That first year," he said, "you'd tell people you played for the Patriots, and they'd ask, 'Who?' In those days, the Giants were the favorite team in New England. They had all the household names—Frank Gifford, Andy Robustelli, Y.A. Tittle, Sam Huff. But slowly but surely we started getting our own fans."

At the outset, many of the Patriots didn't know each other. "We must have gone through a couple hundred players that first year," Cappelletti said. "There was so much confusion that one guy stayed in camp three or four days after he was cut, until one of the coaches caught him loading up his tray in the lunch line."

Tom Yewcic, who was a quarterback and punter for the Pats from 1961 to 1966 and like Cappelletti later became an assistant coach, remembered, "We used to joke about the three teams at the Patriots' camp—one going to the airport with the players just released, another arriving from the airport with a new bunch, and the one on the practice field. You made sure not to get to know anybody real well."

That wasn't too hard to do.

"My first four games," said Yewcic, "the guys who had lockers on either side of me changed every game. That was eight new guys in four games."

But it wasn't long before the Patriots had some recognizable names—and some unforgettable characters.

Ike

Larry "Ike" Eisenhauer, a wild and crazy—and also talented and tenacious—6'5", 250-pound defensive end out of Boston College, played nine years (1961–1969) for the Patriots and was voted to the AFL All-Star Game four times. But it's for his off-field exploits that Eisenhauer is best remembered.

Larry Eisenhauer, pictured here in 1961, had a reputation for eccentric behavior while with the Patriots.

"I wouldn't have been playing for Bill Belichick today," he said, laughing over the phone from the deck of the 60-foot yacht on which he spends the winters in Jupiter, Florida. "I wouldn't have been happy, and he certainly wouldn't have been happy."

Eisenhauer was one of a kind, which, depending on your point of view, is either fortunate or a tragedy.

"In 1963," he said, "we beat the Buffalo Bills in a playoff game and went out to San Diego for the league championship game. The team always stayed in the Stardust Hotel.

"In those days, when we went out to California during the regular season, we'd play the Raiders and Chargers back-to-back and stay out there for the week. Now if you're going to be on the West Coast for a week, you sure as heck don't want to stay in Oakland, so we used to beg Coach [Mike] Holovak to stay in San Diego. Everybody loved the weather, and there were some great beach bars—not to mention the beautiful women.

"My father, Dutch, had always gone to my games, from the time I was in high school on Long Island, through my years at Boston College, and with the Patriots. When he told me he wanted to come out to see the AFL Championship Game, I asked him if he'd like to be my roommate. That made Coach Holovak happy because he probably figured I'd behave myself.

"I had a reputation for being a bit bizarre as far as behavior was concerned—both on and off the field. I had a different roommate every year, both in college and the pros. I wore them all out," Eisenhauer continued.

"Anyway, my dad, who was a big man—6'2" or 6'3", about 265 pounds—came out to San Diego, and after practice we'd relax by the swimming pool in the afternoon. One day, as the sun was starting to go down, I said to him, 'You know, Dad, it's getting a little chilly here, but there's a heated, private pool up on top of the building you might enjoy.' What he didn't know was that the pool I was talking about was actually a tank with a glass wall that was behind the hotel bar where, during cocktail hour, some good-looking girls would perform a water ballet that the guys always enjoyed watching.

"So I take my father up there, and he jumps in and starts swimming around. He's having a ball. I decided to jump in with him. Guys are sitting at the bar waiting to see the girls, and instead they see the two of us. Show business being what it is, a few other players wanted to get into the act. Then the girls showed up and wondered what the heck was going on. That's when management threatened to call the cops and we decided it was time to get out of the pool.

"To set the record straight, the story became, over time, that not only were we in the pool, but we didn't have suits on. My dad became very upset about that." The thing is, for anyone who knew Eisenhauer, it wouldn't have been surprising if he had decided to go skinny-dipping.

"One time we were playing the Chiefs in a late-season game in Kansas City," he said. "It was freezing cold. I put on my cleats and socks, my jock, and a helmet and walked out of the locker room and about halfway up the tunnel to the field. Not all the way out, mind you—just halfway. Nobody in the stands could see me. It was a big game for us, and I did it just to loosen everybody up. Guys were laughing their tails off."

What his teammates didn't always find so amusing were Eisenhauer's methods of getting pumped up before games.

"I'd put on my shoulder pads and slam into my locker a few times," he said. "The story got out that I used to hit it with my head, but that's not true. When we'd go out on the field and we'd be waiting to be introduced, I'd get 10 feet away from the goal post and run into it a couple of times. When I'd do that, guys on the other team would look at me kind of funny.

"Then, when I was introduced, I'd run as fast as I could right to our bench and hit one of our linemen—hard. The guys got a little tired of that. In 1964 we drafted Len St. Jean [who was voted one of the guards on the Patriots' 10th-anniversary team]. The guys told him, 'When Ike comes running over here, we want you to nail him.' So he stepped up and gave me a shot. I smiled at him and said, 'Now we're ready.'"

The Patriots practiced in those days at a high school field in East Boston, near Logan Airport.

"We'd sit on milk crates and watch game films shown on sheets hung on the walls of the locker room," Eisenhauer said.

One day the Patriots were visited at their practice field by Rex Trailer, a singing cowboy who hosted a children's show on one of the Boston television stations. He had a small sidekick known as Pancho, who was going to be filmed wearing a little helmet and running through the Patriots defense for a touchdown as players took pratfalls trying to tackle him.

"I stationed myself at the 10-yard line," Eisenhauer said, chuckling. "Now, I've got all my equipment on, and Pancho, the little goofball, is carrying the football as guys are falling down all around him. He gets near the goal line and I come up on him from the blind side and blast him. I knock him tail over tea kettle. As he's on the ground, wondering what the heck hit him, I look into the camera and say, 'Nobody scores on the Patriots.'"

Nobody ever could predict what Eisenhauer would do next. There was, for instance, the time wide receiver Jimmy Colclough got on the team bus wearing a sports jacket louder than some of the crowds the Patriots played in front of.

"That," Eisenhauer bellowed, "is the ugliest coat I have ever seen!" With that, Eisenhauer grabbed the back of Colclough's collar and tore the jacket all the way down the back.

While his teammates laughed and Colclough stood dumbfounded—he only weighed 185 pounds and was well aware of Eisenhauer's reputation— Eisenhauer quickly reached into his pocket and handed over a $100 bill to pay for a new jacket.

Sometimes his teammates had to pay for Eisenhauer's pranks. Like the time they flew to Rochester to play the Buffalo Bills in a preseason game. Because the game was at night, the Patriots flew up that morning to avoid the cost of an overnight stay. They did, however, spend a few hours that afternoon relaxing at a hotel, where they were warned not to get under the covers of the beds in their rooms—an infraction that would draw a fine of $10.

"What you have to understand," Eisenhauer said, "is that our per diem in those days was $10. We were supposed to pay for three meals out of that, which you could do because you could get breakfast for about $1.50 and lunch for $2.50. So 10 bucks was a pretty stiff fine at the time."

The situation seemed silly to Eisenhauer, who decided to have a few laughs. "I ran around the hotel," he said, "knocking on everybody's door. As soon as they opened up, I'd run past them, pull the covers off the bed, and run out. They didn't know what to say."

Then there was the time Eisenhauer and Charlie Long, an offensive guard who played for the Pats from 1961 to 1969, got in a heated dispute over a program in the locker room before a game. "He was looking at it," Eisenhauer said, "and I asked if I could see it. He said, 'No, I'm reading it.' So I waited. And waited a while longer. I knew he was trying to irritate me, so I ripped it out of his hands.

"With that, he jumped up and took a swing at me. I swung back at him. Tommy Addison [a linebacker who played from 1960 to 1967] stepped in between us to try to break things up, and Charlie decked him with a punch.

"I'll tell you, we had a ball in those days."

Harpo

When Bob Gladieux, a running back who had been cocaptain at Notre Dame and was an eighth-round pick of the Patriots in 1969, failed to survive the final cut at training camp in 1970, he decided to hold his own Irish wake.

Nicknamed "Harpo" after one of the Marx Brothers because of his frizzy blond hair and crazy antics, Gladieux knew how to have a good time.

"I went downtown," he said, "to have a little libation and do a little dancing. I met a fun young lady. We rocked and rolled all that night and then the next two. We had a blast. We partied, and I got rid of my frustration.

"On the Sunday morning of the season opener against the Dolphins, I woke up somewhere on Beacon Hill and, all of a sudden, I got sentimental. I thought, *I've got to go out to Harvard Stadium and see the guys play*. A friend came by to pick me up. I had a six pack of tall 16-ounce beers. He brought a bottle of wine. When we got to the stadium, I bought a program, showed an usher my picture, told him the story of what happened to me, and he let me in for free. So we go in, and I tell my buddy, 'You get the first round, I'll get the second. And don't forget the mustard on my hot dog!'

"He'd gone to the concession stand when I suddenly hear, 'Bob Gladieux please report to the Patriots' dressing room!' I thought I was dreaming. I look up, and I swear it was a blue-grey sky, just like in the story Grantland Rice wrote about the Four Horsemen. I look up at the sky, and it's like God is telling me to report.

"But then I think, *Maybe He's punishing me for being mischievous.* That's when the lightbulb went off in my head. And it had a dollar sign on it. I said to myself, 'Do it for the money, you fool.'

Bob Gladieux, pictured here in 1969, was nicknamed Harpo because of his curly hair and zany antics.

"So I dart out of the stands and down to the locker room. I was in no condition to play, but Clive [Rush, the head coach] says, 'You're activated. Get dressed.'

"I've got about five minutes to get my pads and uniform on and get out on the field. I'm still tying my britches when they send me out to cover the kickoff. Normally I'd be saying to myself, 'Okay, go down and bust the hell out of the wedge and make the tackle.' Instead I'm thinking, *Whatever you do, Harpo, protect yourself. Avoid all contact. Don't get hurt.*

"We kick off, and as I head down the field the wedge is coming straight at me. Now, while I'm running, my buddy has come back to our seats with our beer and hot dogs. He's asking people, 'Where's the guy who was sitting here?' They told him I'd left, and he was wondering: 'Where the hell did Harpo go now?'

"Meanwhile, I want nothing to do with the wedge, so I run around it to the left side. The ball carrier went around the right side and ran right into my arms. That's when my buddy hears the public address announcer say, 'Tackle by No. 24, Bob Gladieux.'

"I think he spilled the beer."

Perhaps inspired by Harpo's heroics, the Patriots went on to defeat the Dolphins 27–14. It would turn out to be one of only two wins they had that season.

Gino

"He was our first superstar."

That's how Patrick Sullivan, Billy's youngest son and general manager of the Patriots from 1983 through 1990, describes Gino Cappelletti.

"He was a great player. And he's such a special man."

That he was. And that he is.

As a player Cappelletti ranks as the AFL's all-time scoring leader, with 1,100 points. In addition to being the Patriots' kicker, he also was one of the team's leading receivers. He was the league MVP in 1964, led the league in scoring five times, and is one of only three players to have appeared in every game in the AFL's 10-year history.

What's really amazing about that is, when Cappelletti showed up for the Patriots' first training camp in the summer of 1960 at the University of Massachusetts, he didn't know if he'd be around long enough to play in even one game.

"Nobody knew," he said, "if the league was going to make it, if the franchise was going to make it, if we'd ever play a game."

Nor did Cappelletti know if he'd make the team.

He'd been a quarterback in college at Minnesota, but that was in the Gophers' single-wing offense, which featured All-American tailback Paul Giel, who went on to play for the Giants—the San Francisco Giants that is—as a pitcher.

Cappelletti couldn't throw a football or a baseball very well.

"I had a tryout with the Detroit Lions as a quarterback," he said. "But they had Bobby Layne, and I didn't have a big arm. I didn't get to stick around long enough to show them what I could do as a kicker."

So Cappelletti did a hitch in the army, after which he played briefly in Canada. He was working as a bartender in Minneapolis when he convinced Lou Saban—the Patriots' first coach, who remembered him from their days in the Big 10 when Saban was coaching at Northwestern—to allow him to come to training camp.

Among those who showed up that first year, Cappelletti recalled, were former NFL players such as hard-hitting linebacker Hardy Brown, who had been a popular player with the 49ers, and an offensive lineman named Gunner Gatski.

"Gatski looked like somebody's grandfather," Cappelletti said. "But we heard he had once been a great center with the Cleveland Browns."

As for Brown, "He wasn't really big enough to play quarterback in a peewee league. Still, he was hurting people all the time. He was a vicious hitter. "We had a lot of old-timers in that first camp," Cappelletti said. "But [Saban] soon found out that they couldn't stay with the younger guys."

Cappelletti wasn't an old-timer, by any means, but he certainly wasn't one of the younger guys, either. He knew this would be his last chance to play pro ball, and he'd have to make the most of it. He also knew that if Saban got a look at his weak arm, he'd never take a look at him as a kicker. So he decided to try to make the team as a defensive back.

"I had played a little defense in college," he said, "and I'd always had the knack of being around the ball. Also I wasn't afraid to hit. I knew every coach likes hitters, and I figured that if I threw my body around I had a chance of lasting at least until they started looking for a kicker. "Kicking was my pride and joy. I loved doing it. Even as a kid, every team I was on I wanted to be the kicker." It's a testament to Cappelletti's athleticism—and admittedly, perhaps also to the lack of top-flight talent available—that he not only made the team as a defensive back, but he also set a club record that still stands (although he shares it now) by intercepting three passes in one game against the Raiders.

He scored the first points in AFL history—booting a 35-yard field goal in the first quarter of a Friday night game against Denver at B.U. Field that the Broncos came back to win 13–10—and, as he would every season through 1969, he finished the year as the Patriots' scoring leader.

Cappelletti knew, however, he wouldn't stick around very long as a defensive back and, with only 33 players on the roster, most teams couldn't afford the luxury of a player whose sole job was kicking field goals and extra points.

Clearly, he figured, it was time for another position change. When injuries left the Patriots' receiving corps shorthanded early the following season, Cappelletti saw his opportunity.

"One day in practice," he said, "we were down to two guys because of injuries. One time, they were slow getting back—they were getting tired, running every route—and I was standing behind the huddle. Butch Songin, our quarterback, started calling the play, even though there was a hole in the huddle, so I jumped in.

"He called a pass pattern. I knew it and ran it. Butch, without even thinking, threw the ball to me, and I caught it. Mike Holovak, who was still the receivers coach then, stopped me as I was going back to the huddle and asked where I had learned to catch the ball.

"I told him I'd caught some passes in college. That's when he told me, 'You stay out with me after practice. We need help at that position.'"

Cappelletti proved to be much better at catching passes than defending them. He finished that 1961 season as the Patriots' leading receiver, with 45 catches for 768 yards and eight touchdowns. Combined with his 17 field goals and 48 PATs, Cappelletti racked up 147 points and led the league in scoring.

His career-high point total—and still the Patriots' all-time single-season scoring record—came in 1964, when he scored 155 points on seven touchdowns, a two-point conversion, 25 field goals, and 36 PATs. He also led the team in receptions that year with 49 for 865 yards. Is it any wonder he was the AFL's MVP that season?

Although he didn't have a strong arm, Cappelletti had a powerful leg. The 53-yard field goal he booted against the Jets in 1965 stood for 25 years as the longest in team history until Jason Staurovsky equaled it in 1990. The club record now belongs to Super Bowl hero Adam Vinatieri, who hit a 57-yarder against the Bears in 2002.

The 2009 season is the 50th for the Patriots. Cappelletti has been around the franchise for 42 of them—11 as a player, three as an assistant coach under Ron Erhardt, and the last 28 as color analyst on the team's radio broadcasts.

As Pat Sullivan says, "Gino is such a special man."

Of all the stadiums the Patriots called home during their nomadic days of the '60s, Fenway Park was Cappelletti's favorite.

"Playing in Fenway," he said, "gave us the feeling of being truly professional. We dressed in the Red Sox's clubhouse, where Ted Williams and so many great players had been. And when we went out on the field, it was like being in the heart of Boston. It meant a lot to us."

It was because the football fans in New England were beginning to take the Patriots to heart that the team moved from B.U. Field to Fenway. "Fenway had more capacity," Pat Sullivan said. "We could seat 36,000 for football."

Among the memories they took with them was the tale of the man in the trench coat. "It was 1961 and we were playing the Dallas Texans," Cappelletti said. "We had a big crowd—more than 25,000. The score was 28–21, but Dallas was driving toward the tying touchdown in the final seconds of the game. Chris Burford caught a pass and got tackled at the 1-yard line. People thought the game was over and came out of the stands and on to the field to celebrate. But the official said there was still one second left.

"So they get everybody off the field, except now the fans are standing all along the sidelines and behind the end zones. The Texans have one more play, and they try to throw to Burford again in the end zone, but some guy comes running out of the pack and gets right in front of him. The ball went through Burford's hands, the guy ran back into the crowd, and the game was over. It was hilarious."

At Fenway, the best seats in the house were bleachers set up in front of the famous left-field wall, the Green Monster. The benches for both teams also were on that side of the field, in close proximity to the fans.

"Our coach, Mike Holovak, never swore," Sullivan said. "Sid Gillman, who was coach of the Chargers, would come in and every other word was an obscenity. The referee one day was a Holy Cross graduate, but Gillman thought he had gone to Boston College, where Holovak had played. The Chargers were getting a lot of penalties, and Gillman was all over the guy, calling him every name in the book, telling him he knew he was 'in the tank.'

"Finally, Holovak walked to the end of our bench, near where the Chargers were, and said, 'Sidney, your language is not appropriate!'

"After the games," said Sullivan, "the fans used to walk on the field and mingle with the players. The atmosphere was very informal. Some of the guys used to get dates that way.

"One afternoon, after a game against Buffalo, an older, white-haired guy walked out of the stands and up to the Bills' quarterback, Jack Kemp. He was one of our season-ticket holders, and he told Kemp that he was a good-looking guy, like Jack Kennedy, with charisma and obvious leadership ability. He said he thought Kemp might have a future in politics after he was finished with football."

Kemp was, as it turned out, interested in politics. He led the Bills to the league championship in 1964 and 1965 and retired after the 1969 season. Two years later, he was elected to Congress from a district in Buffalo and served nine terms in the House of Representatives. He also was considered as a candidate for president and ran as the Republican vice-presidential candidate in 1996.

"I met Congressman Kemp years later," Sullivan said, "and he told me the man he'd talked to that day never forgave him because he ran as a Republican. When I asked him why, he said, 'Because the man was Tip O'Neill.'"

O'Neill was, of course, a prominent Democrat who served 34 years in Congress and was Speaker of the House for 10 years, from 1977 until his retirement in 1987.

The Patriots' quarterback in those days was Vito "Babe" Parilli, who'd been a collegiate star at Kentucky when Bear Bryant was coaching the Wildcats and was a first-round pick of the Packers in 1952. But he had been primarily a backup in Green Bay and was playing in the Canadian Football League when the AFL was formed. He returned to the States to play for the Raiders in 1960, the league's first season, after which he was traded to the Patriots.

"Babe was kind of fidgety and nervous," Cappelletti said, "but he was very adept once he took the snap from center. He could throw the ball. He had a nice touch, and he was always a student of the game."

It was with Parilli at quarterback that the Patriots played in their only AFL Championship Game, in 1963. As it turned out, it wasn't much of a game as the Chargers rolled to a 51–10 romp in San Diego.

"They had a great offensive team," Cappelletti said. "They had guys like Keith Lincoln [who ran for 206 yards and a touchdown on just 13 carries and also caught seven passes for 123 yards and another touchdown], Paul Lowe, Lance Alworth, and John Hadl.

"We were a blitzing team. We'd blitz, blitz, and then blitz again. We'd gotten by that way the whole year. All the Chargers did was throw short passes when our guys were blitzing, and there was nobody to make the tackle."

The Patriots were 10–3–1 the following year but lost the Eastern Division title to the Bills. When Holovak and the Pats went 3–10–1 in 1967 and 4–10 in '68, Billy Sullivan decided it was time to make a coaching change.

The problem was, he made the wrong decision.

The man he really wanted was Chuck Noll, the defensive backfield coach for Don Shula in Baltimore, where the Colts had won the 1968 NFL championship. Also in the running for the job was Clive Rush, the receivers coach for Weeb Ewbank's AFL champion New York Jets. When the Jets, led by colorful quarterback Joe Namath, upset the Colts in Super Bowl III, Sullivan was faced with a dilemma.

"There was always so much negative press about the Patriots playing in a 'Mickey Mouse League,'" Sullivan said. "I was concerned that, if we hired Noll, the headlines would be along the lines of 'Losing Super Bowl Coach Hired by Patriots.'

"It was a dumb decision on my part to base it on that because Noll actually impressed me more than Rush. Then again, if Noll had come in here and been 1–13, the way he was his first year in Pittsburgh, he probably would have been run out of town."

As it was, Noll won four Super Bowls with the Steelers while Clive lasted only a season and a half in Boston.

But what a season and a half it was.

Clive

The reason the Patriots put out an emergency call for Bob "Harpo" Gladieux the afternoon of their 1970 season opener at Harvard Stadium was that Clive Rush, their eccentric coach, impulsively cut two players that morning.

Rush was hired in the midst of a five-year stretch during which the Patriots changed coaches even more often than they changed playing fields, going from Mike Holovak to Rush to John Mazur and then to Phil Bengston—before Chuck Fairbanks arrived in 1973 and ended the chaos in the coach's office. At least until he threw things into turmoil by bailing on the Patriots for the University of Colorado in 1978.

Rush's brief tenure in Boston did not get off to a propitious start. To begin with, the flight he was scheduled to take from New York to get to his introductory press conference was cancelled because of bad weather, so he had to come up to Boston on the train.

"That's the first time," he quipped, "I've ever heard of a coach being ridden *into* town on a rail."

On November 3, 1970, the Patriots announced that head coach Clive Rush had been placed on an indefinite leave of absence for health reasons. But Rush told the media that he had quit the club at midnight the night before and said, "I will never coach this football team again!" Photo courtesy of AP Images.

Rush wasn't laughing at another press conference a few days later when he took the microphone to introduce the team's new general manager, George Sauer Jr., who also had been hired away from the Jets.

"As soon as Clive touched the microphone, he screeched," recalled Ron Hobson, the congenial sportswriter who covered the Patriots for the evening newspaper in Quincy, Massachusetts—coincidentally called the *Patriot Ledger*—from the earliest days of the franchise until his retirement in 2008.

"What hair he had on the sides of his head went out in little puff-balls," Hobson said. "He froze. Couldn't move. Somebody ran and pulled the plug, and Clive slumped to the floor."

Shocked by a short circuit, Rush quickly recovered.

"When he stood up again," Hobson said, "that's when he uttered his most famous line: 'I heard the Boston press was tough, but this is ridiculous.'"

Ridiculousness occurred with regularity when Rush was coaching the Patriots—in part because he drank often, and early.

"I knew we had a problem," said Jon Morris, "when Clive said he needed to talk with me and Houston Antwine—he was the defensive captain, I was the offensive captain—and asked if we could come to his office early the next morning.

"We showed up at 8:00 and, when we sat down, he reaches into his desk drawer and pulls out a bottle of Scotch and three glasses and says, 'Want to join me?'"

Perhaps it was after a few pops that Rush conceived the idea of a "Black Power Defense."

Black Power was a popular concept during the Civil Rights movement of the late '60s, and Rush, feeling the Patriots needed an emotional lift in addition to some improvement defensively, decided to assemble a unit comprised entirely of African American players.

The problem was that, in order to do so, he had to shift some offensive players to defense in order to fill every position.

"Everybody on the team, including the black guys, thought he was nuts," said Patrick Sullivan.

Rush quickly became more than a little paranoid.

"I remember a team meeting," said Morris, "when Clive was on a rant. We had lost the last several games, and Clive was beginning to come unglued because the local press was getting on his case. Several players had been quoted anonymously with some snide comments regarding the coach's approach to things, so Clive felt it was time to lecture us on how to handle the newspaper guys.

"So he's going on about the evils of the media, how all they want to do is destroy us, they never have their facts straight, and so on, ad nauseam. Finally, he says we must be careful because 'The pen is mightier than the sword,' and so we're in no position to fight back.

"Mike Taliaferro, who was our quarterback and therefore seated in the front row, raises his hand and asks, 'Who said that? Who said the pen is mightier than the sword?'

"This gets a good laugh as Clive's jaw drops to the floor. But he recovers quickly, announcing that he knows the answer but is willing to bet that no one else in the room does. Whereupon he says that he will cut practice short by one hour if anyone knows the answer.

"Larry Carwell, a defensive back, immediately leaps out of his seat and shouts, 'Cardinal Richelieu!' Clive turns white, unable to believe that a defensive back would know this. To make matters even more hilarious, Carwell goes on to say that Richelieu did not actually say this line, but that it was used by an actor portraying the cardinal in an 1839 stage play written by Edward Bulwer-Lytton. Really, this is all true. I'm not making this up.

"So Carwell sits down—to a standing ovation from the rest of us— and Clive has no choice but to tell us that practice will be cut short by an hour. Which, frankly, was probably the last thing we needed at that stage of the season.

"From then on, Carwell was affectionately known as Cardinal Carwell."

Jon Morris

He may have been the best player the Patriots had in their early years, and the only reason they got him was that he wasn't sure he was all that good.

Jon Morris was a second-round draft pick of the Green Bay Packers in 1964 when the Pack, coached by the legendary Vince Lombardi, was coming off an 11–2–1 season after having been NFL champions in 1961 and 1962.

The Patriots, who'd just lost in the AFL Championship Game to San Diego, didn't pick him until the fourth round.

A standout at center and linebacker for Holy Cross, the 6'4", 250-pound Morris was selected to play in both the Senior Bowl and the College All-Star Game in Chicago, against the NFL champion Bears.

Without question, he was one of the top prospects among offensive linemen in the 1963 draft. But Morris questioned whether he could play for Lombardi and the Packers.

"Honestly," he says now, looking back on his decision to sign with the Patriots, "I didn't have the self-confidence to play for the Packers. I didn't think I was good enough.

"Lombardi called me on the phone. He said he'd give me a two-year, no-cut contract and told me that Jim Ringo wasn't going to be there. But I figured that was just 'coach talk.' I knew [Patriots coach] Mike Holovak. There was a comfort factor involved."

Jon Morris, shown here on July 30, 1973, joined the Patriots because he didn't think he was good enough to play for the Packers, who offered him a contract first. Photo courtesy of AP Images.

Lombardi was being straight with Morris. Ringo, who'd been Green Bay's starting center since 1953 and had played in seven Pro Bowls, was traded to Philadelphia before the 1964 season, in part because he'd brought an agent with him to discuss contract terms with Lombardi. Ringo went on to play four seasons with the Eagles, going to three more Pro Bowls, and was elected to the Pro Football Hall of Fame in 1981.

With a no-cut contract, Morris likely would have taken Ringo's place in Green Bay. As it was, the job went to Ken Bowman, picked in the eighth round that same year, 1964, out of Wisconsin. Bowman was more than capable, playing for a decade and earning a spot in the Packers Hall of Fame.

"Everybody has their 'what if' moment in life," Morris said. "Look what likely would have happened if I'd gone to Green Bay. I probably would have played in one of the most famous games of all time—the Ice Bowl against Dallas for the NFL championship in 1967. The Packers won three straight NFL championships from '65 through '67 and won the first two Super Bowls.

"On the other hand, I would have had to live in Green Bay, and I'd never have met my wife."

Morris and his wife of more than 40 years, Gail, have retired to South Carolina. But they spent most of their lives in Massachusetts, where Jon played 11 seasons for the Patriots from 1964 through 1974. Traded to Detroit in 1975, he played three years with the Lions, then one for the Bears.

Once he quit playing he returned to the greater Boston area and kept his hand—or his voice, to be more accurate—in football. He signed on as the color analyst on the Patriots' radio broadcasts in 1978 and handled that assignment for 10 years, working with Gil Santos and John Carlson.

"I enjoyed it," Morris said. "Coming to the stadium every Sunday and not getting hit in the head was wonderful."

He was succeeded in the booth by another Patriots legend, Gino Cappelletti, who has had the job ever since.

Morris tells a funny story about how, when Cappelletti was an assistant coach on Ron Erhardt's staff in New England, Cappelletti tipped him off to something that would make him sound very smart on the radio.

"We were riding together on the team bus to a game in Buffalo," Morris recalled, "and Gino said to me, 'When's the last time you saw the Patriots try a fake field goal?'

"I said, 'Never.' 'Well, he said, we're going to do it today. Keep your eye on me. I'll raise my right hand and wave at you when we're ready to try it.'

"I thought that was fabulous," Morris said. "I was going to look like a genius.

"John Carlson was doing the play-by-play then, and he was talking when, as the Patriots sent their field-goal unit on to the field, I saw Gino wave at me. But Carlson wouldn't stop talking, and I couldn't cut him off.

"Sure enough, the Patriots tried a fake. Of course, being the Patriots, it didn't work."

Morris surely would have had much more success playing for the Pack than he had with the Pats, who, after going 10–3–1 his rookie year in '64, had only one more winning season the last 10 years he was there, and that was in 1966, when they were 8–4–2.

Morris was one of the few bright spots in an otherwise largely dismal Patriots picture. For six straight years, from 1964 through 1969, he was selected to play in the AFL All-Star Game. In 1970 he was voted to the NFL Pro Bowl. He was the Patriots' only representative that year, and they didn't have another until 1976, when John Hannah, Mike Haynes, Russ Francis, and Leon Gray all were selected.

"I always thought things were going to get better," Morris said. "But they never did."

chapter 3

Homes Sweet Homes

After six seasons at Fenway Park, the Patriots had worn out both the field—"They wanted us to pay to replace it," Patrick Sullivan said—and their welcome. So, in 1969, they moved again—this time to Billy Sullivan's alma mater, Boston College.

Sullivan, who had grown up in the industrial city of Lowell, north of Boston, where his father was a newspaperman, graduated from Boston College in 1937. The following year he convinced the Jesuits to hire him as the school's first full-time sports (and public) information director.

"They thought public relations weren't dignified," Sullivan said, "until I pointed out that Harvard had a whole department to project the university's image."

In the "timing is everything department," Frank Leahy, who had played for the legendary Knute Rockne at Notre Dame, arrived at Boston College shortly after Sullivan, having been lured away from Fordham to take over as the Eagles' football coach.

Leahy was so successful—he led Boston College to an undefeated season in 1940, capped by a victory in the Sugar Bowl over Tennessee—that he was hired by Notre Dame. Accompanying him to South Bend was the young Billy Sullivan.

They remained friends for the rest of their lives, and Leahy was instrumental in helping Sullivan obtain a franchise in the fledgling American Football League.

While the Patriots made it through that 1969 season without incident—and without many victories (they finished 4–10)—their final game at Alumni Stadium almost turned into a disaster.

Although they had made arrangements to play at Harvard Stadium in 1970, the Patriots played their only home preseason game that year at Boston College. It was against the Redskins and in the midst of the action that radio announcer Gil Santos smelled smoke wafting toward the press box.

"The radio booth was right on top of the stands, which at that time were wooden bleachers," he said. "I saw people down below me starting to scatter. Then I saw smoke, followed by a mad dash of fans running down, out of the bleachers, right on to the field.

"Smoke was billowing up. Flames were shooting up. The referee stopped the game. Our booth was wooden, so I'm thinking, *If the stands are on fire, there's a good chance this booth will catch fire, too.*"

But the quick-thinking Santos didn't abandon his post immediately.

"One of our sponsors at the time," he said, "was Narragansett Beer. They had a series of television commercials in which the punch line was, 'But first, I'll have one more 'Gansett.' As I'm describing how the flames are shooting up, and the stands are burning, and that we're about to go off the air, I said, 'But first, I'll have one more 'Gansett.'

"As it turned out, we never did leave the booth. The firemen arrived on the scene very quickly, and it didn't take them long to put the fire out."

The cause of the smoky blaze was a popcorn machine in a concession stand beneath the bleachers.

"Fortunately," Santos said, "nobody was hurt, and it wasn't a huge section of seats that were burned. After the fire was out, everybody found a seat, and the game continued. Popcorn sales, of course, were down."

Gino Cappelletti, Santos' longtime partner on the Patriots' game-day radio broadcasts, was then one of the stars of the team.

"We didn't know what was happening," Cappelletti said, "until the fans started to come on to the field. Then we saw the smoke and flames in the stands. We were standing around on the field, and fans started coming up to us, putting their arms around our shoulder pads. They were talking to the Washington guys, too. Everybody was asking, 'Hey, how you doin'? What town are you from? Isn't this something?'"

"It was funny," said Santos, "to see the fans out on the field, hobnobbing with the players. They were all standing around together, talking and watching the fire."

The Patriots were happy to move to the larger Harvard Stadium.

"My father's desire, from the start of the franchise, was to play at Harvard," Patrick Sullivan said. "It was the best facility."

Unfortunately Harvard did not deign to allow the Patriots full use of its facilities. The team was provided with just one locker room—the one used by visiting college teams. The Patriots gave it to their visitors because it would have been both unacceptable and unconscionable to make their opponents dress in the Ramada Inn, across several athletic fields from the stadium, as the Patriots had to do.

"That would have been tough to explain," Sullivan said, chuckling.

Meanwhile the Patriots were under increasing pressure to finally find a permanent home. The terms of the merger agreement between the NFL and AFL required all teams to have a stadium seating at least 50,000.

Billy Sullivan, after many false starts and false hopes, believed he was on the verge of resolving the Patriots' stadium problems when a proposal for a domed stadium to be built along the Neponset River, near the city line with Quincy, was under serious discussion in the Boston City Council.

But Ron Hobson, a sportswriter for the *Quincy Patriot-Ledger*, had a friend on the council who told him in no uncertain terms that there never would be a football stadium built in the city because no neighborhood would accept it.

Thinking about possibilities outside of Boston, Hobson had an idea. In addition to his newspaper work, he also was the publicity director for Bay State Raceway, a harness track on Route 1 in Foxboro, less than 30 minutes south of the city, about halfway between Boston and Providence, Rhode Island.

The track was owned by E.M. Loew, who had made his fortune in movie theaters. It was set back from the highway and was surrounded by open land.

"I called Billy," said Hobson, who had been covering the Patriots since their first season, "and he came down for a visit. The track employees were given the day off so they wouldn't see him touring the site. He'd always been adamant about building in the city of Boston, and there had been a number of proposals over the years. But he fell in love with the idea."

Sullivan was able to get a stadium seating 61,297 built for what now seems like the laughably low sum of $6.7 million. But that didn't mean the Patriots' stadium woes were over.

The first game was played in the new facility on August 15, 1971. It was a preseason game against the New York Giants and the official attendance was listed as 60,423.

But the fact is, many of the people who tried to get to the game never got into the parking lots, much less the stadium.

Route 1 through Foxboro is only four lanes, two in each direction, and it had never seen the volume of traffic that poured into town that night.

"Looking up and down Route 1 from the press box," Santos recalled, "I could see a seemingly endless line of car headlights. And it never seemed to move.

"There was no room in the parking lots," he said. "It was a disaster. I still run into people who tell me they heard the entire game on the radio while sitting in their cars within sight of the stadium."

Those who did get to their seats and saw the Patriots win 20–14 found that all the kinks had not yet been worked out in the new facility. There were some plumbing issues. Because of a dispute with the union, some urinals were placed so high that only men who were at least six feet tall could use them. Patriots wide receiver Randy Vataha, who was only 5'8", complained that he couldn't use the facilities in the locker room unless one of his teammates held him up.

There also were some questions about water pressure. The Foxboro town fathers were worried that if a fire broke out in town while a game was going on, there might not be enough pressure to extinguish the flames.

With the next home game two weeks away, the club worked feverishly to resolve the problems. The day before the Patriots were to take on the Rams, a test was held that is fondly remembered by all participants as the Big Flush.

"It was the funniest thing I experienced in all my years with the Patriots," said Santos, who was one of several media members recruited to participate in a stadium-wide drill in which all the toilets and urinals would be flushed at approximately the same time.

"It was set up like a military operation," Santos said. "We were divided into platoons and stationed all along the concourse level. Each of us was assigned a bathroom. We stood at the entrance of our designated restroom, poised and ready for action.

"There were people with whistles and, when they blew them, we had been instructed to run into every men's room, every ladies' room, turn on the faucets and flush every urinal, every toilet, as fast as we could. When the whistles blew, off we went, flushing like mad and laughing like hell.

"When it was over, they announced the operation had been a success."

It was one of the few successes the Patriots had in those days, when they were in the midst of a nine-year stretch without a winning season.

chapter 4

Talented Teams

The Fairbanks Years

What may have been the most talented of all Patriots teams not only never won a Super Bowl, they never even won a playoff game. Although those teams coached by Chuck Fairbanks from 1976 through 1978 did win a division title.

His 1976 team lost the season opener and then won 11 of 13—including an eye-opening, confidence-building 30–27 victory in Pittsburgh in Week 3 as well as their last six in a row. But having to travel to Oakland as the wild-card team (Baltimore won the AFC East on a tiebreaker), the Patriots lost in the final minute to the Raiders, 24–21, in a game they felt the officials took away from them.

The 1977 season was marred by the holdouts of All-Pro offensive linemen John Hannah and Leon Gray, the most dominating left side in the league. They sat out the first two games and weren't really ready when they took the field in Week 3, and so the Patriots started out 1–2 and wound up stumbling to a 9–5 record that wasn't good enough for a playoff spot.

The NFL went to a 16-game schedule in 1978, and the Patriots already had clinched the division title when they took an 11–4 record to Miami for the season finale. But the high hopes they had for postseason success were dashed by one of the more bizarre incidents in a team history filled with strange occurrences.

Success had been in short supply in New England prior to the arrival of Fairbanks from the University of Oklahoma, where he'd had back-to-back 11–1 seasons capped by two straight Sugar Bowl victories.

Chuck Fairbanks, right, discusses a play with quarterback Steve Grogan during a workout on December 15, 1976, at Schaefer Stadium as they prepared for a playoff game against the Oakland Raiders. Fairbanks' teams of the 1970s were arguably some of the best teams in Patriots history. Photo courtesy of AP Images.

The Patriots hadn't had a winning season since 1966, when they went 8–4–2 under Mike Holovak. Although well-liked and respected by players and management, Holovak was fired after the 1968 season, when the Pats were 4–10, after having gone 3–10–1 in 1967.

Unfortunately his replacement was the disastrous Clive Rush. He lasted a season and a half before being replaced by John Mazur. After a 4–12 record in Rush's first year, the Patriots were 2–12 in 1970. They improved to 6–8 in 1971, but when they lost seven of their first nine games the following year, Billy Sullivan fired Mazur. Phil Bengston stepped in as interim coach and completed a 3–11 season.

Having had four coaches in five years, Sullivan was searching for stability when he tried to convince Joe Paterno to leave Penn State and come to New England. Following weeks of negotiations, during which Paterno actually agreed to take the job, he called Sullivan one morning after a sleepless night and said that he had changed his mind. Sullivan made overtures to several other top college coaches—John McKay at Southern Cal, Ara Parseghian at Notre Dame, Darrell Royal at Texas, and Bob Devaney at Nebraska.

Devaney actually came to Foxboro for an interview, during which he asked to look at some game film of the team. While he was watching, one of Mazur's lame-duck assistants came into the room.

"Who's that end?" Devaney inquired.

"That's Rick Cash," the assistant said.

"Boy, he's not a very good player, is he?" Devaney said.

"Hey, Bob," the assistant replied, "if you think Cash is bad, wait 'til you see the rest of the film."

In the end it was Fairbanks who agreed to come, and he didn't waste any time laying the foundation for what would be the most talented teams in Patriots history—even more talented, although obviously nowhere near as successful, as Bill Belichick's Super Bowl–winning squads.

The Patriots accumulated three first-round picks for Fairbanks' first draft in 1973 and hit the jackpot with all of them.

They took future Hall of Fame guard John Hannah with the fourth overall choice; selected fullback Sam "Bam" Cunningham, a bruising blocker and punishing runner, at No. 11; then added wide receiver Darryl Stingley with the 19th pick.

New England didn't have a first-round choice the following year but was able to add linebacker Steve Nelson in Round 2 and running back Andy Johnson in Round 5.

In 1975, thanks to the acumen of superscout Bucko Kilroy, the Patriots picked up tight end Russ Francis—called "all-world" by no less an authority than Howard Cosell—in the first round and quarterback Steve Grogan in the fifth. On the field, however, the Patriots still struggled. They were only 3–11 in 1975, but they were very close to being good. What put them over the top was the Jim Plunkett trade in 1976—a deal that turned out to be the NFL equivalent of a Brinks robbery.

The Heisman Trophy winner at Stanford in 1970, Plunkett had been drafted by New England with the first overall pick in 1971. He was big at 6'4" and 225 pounds and blessed with a strong and accurate arm. But he couldn't move very well, and unfortunately the Patriots had an offensive line that couldn't protect him.

He was thrown immediately into the lineup, starting every game as a rookie, and took a terrible pounding. His second season, battered and harassed, he threw 25 interceptions and only eight touchdown passes.

After five years, during which he was sacked the mind-boggling total of 156 times—and it would have been more, had he not lost his starting job to the rookie Grogan in 1975—Plunkett was begging to get of town and return to his native California, where the 49ers were eager to get him. So eager, as it turned out, that they were willing to part with two first-round picks that year, and first- and second-round choices in 1977. It was a deal the Patriots couldn't refuse.

The trade turned out to be a disaster for the 49ers but worked wonderfully for the Patriots and, in the long run, Plunkett as well. Although he was waived by San Francisco after the 1978 season, he wound up signing with Oakland after sitting out a year and led the Raiders to victory in Super Bowl XV after the 1980 season, a game in which he was the MVP.

With the plethora of picks they obtained from the 49ers for Plunkett, the Patriots added future Hall of Fame cornerback Mike Haynes, center Pete Brock, and safety Tim Fox in the first round in 1976. They then picked up cornerback Raymond Clayborn and explosive wide receiver Stanley Morgan in the first round in 1977.

"Those were the best Patriots teams we ever had," Hannah said. "They had heart. They worked hard. They were great teams."

But they never won the truly big games—the postseason games that determine how a team is remembered. The 1976 team seemed destined for great things when, after losing the opener to Baltimore, they followed a 30–14 mauling of Miami with a stunning 30–27 upset of the defending Super Bowl champion Steelers in Pittsburgh.

The Steelers fumbled seven times in that game, and the Patriots recovered six of them. Grogan threw a 58-yard touchdown pass to Stingley and a 38-yarder to Francis. He also ran six yards for a touchdown, one of 12 he scored that season, setting an NFL record for quarterbacks that appears unlikely to be broken.

"This win," Fairbanks said, "has to be one of the biggest and best in our history."

"It tasted," said Hannah, "like a big chew of tobacco—the kind you savor so much you hate to spit it out."

The Patriots then rolled over the Raiders 48–17 the following Sunday in Foxboro but had a much tougher time in their rematch at Oakland in the playoffs.

Having gone from 3–11 in 1975 to 11–3 in 1976, the Patriots were, in the opinion of many, on their way to their first Super Bowl. Had they gotten there, they very well may have won, since it was the Raiders who were victorious in Super Bowl XI, trouncing Minnesota 32–14. But the Pats were flagged down in Oakland.

Trailing 10–7 at halftime, New England scored two touchdowns in the third quarter and took a 21–10 lead into the final 15 minutes. The Raiders closed to 21–17, but the Patriots appeared to be in good shape when, with less than five minutes to play, they were in a third-and-short situation at the Oakland 28.

But then there was an illegal-motion penalty that put the ball back beyond the 33, and when Grogan tried to throw to Francis on third down, the big tight end was all but tackled by linebacker Phil Villapiano before the ball arrived. The Patriots looked for a flag but didn't get one.

When John Smith's 50-yard field-goal attempt was, not surprisingly, no good (he was a very accurate kicker but didn't have great range), the Raiders were 68 yards from the end zone with 4:12 to go.

Oakland advanced to the New England 19, where the Patriots sacked quarterback Kenny "Snake" Stabler for a loss of eight yards. He threw incomplete on second down and then again on third down.

But wait! There's a late flag thrown by referee Ben Dreith, who said Ray "Sugar Bear" Hamilton was guilty of roughing the passer. Instead of fourth-and-18, the Raiders had a first down at the 12.

That's when the Patriots lost their composure and the game. They drew an unsportsmanlike-conduct penalty, Stabler eventually ran the ball into the end zone himself from the 1-yard line for the winning touchdown, and the Pats again were penalized for unsportsmanlike conduct.

They were frustrated by Dreith's late flag, the noncall when Francis was interfered with, and the fact that center Bill Lenkaitis drew three holding penalties, while Oakland's offensive line wasn't called for any.

"We got robbed," Grogan said, still bitter more than 30 years later. "That team could have won the Super Bowl."

The holdouts by Hannah and Grey proved costly in 1977, but the Patriots were back in synch in 1978, when they literally ran all over the opposition, setting an NFL mark that still stands—and is likely to for a long while—by rushing for 3,165 yards on 671 attempts. Cunningham led the team with 768, Horace Ivory had 693, Andy Johnson totaled 675, and even quarterback Grogan racked up 539.

"It was fun to be part of that," Grogan said. "We'd just run the ball down people's throats."

But the Patriots ran into trouble when it became known that Fairbanks was about to run off to Colorado.

That news broke the day before New England, which already had clinched first place in the division, was to finish the regular season in a Monday-night game at Miami.

Sullivan was, understandably, irate. He decided he would not allow Fairbanks to coach against the Dolphins and appointed the coordinators as co–head coaches. Ron Erhardt would run the offense while Hank Bullough would direct the defense.

"Chuck was in a corner of the locker room with Mr. Sullivan," Nelson said. "Billy wanted him to quit. Chuck wanted to be fired because, that way, he'd have to be paid. It was a huge distraction. It was hard to focus on playing."

"We were stunned," Brock said. "We weren't quite sure how to act. We had two pregame speeches that night—one from Erhardt, one from Bullough."

Not even Knute Rockne could have inspired the Patriots that night.

"I'll never forget that game," cornerback Raymond Clayborn said. "It was our last game of the year and we were ready for the playoffs. All of a sudden we had the coach of the team sitting over in a corner of the locker room and two assistant coaches coaching the team. Guys didn't know whether to laugh or cry. That really hurt us. It took anything we had out of us for the playoffs."

Although Sullivan allowed Fairbanks to coach the playoff game against Houston two weeks later in Foxboro, the Patriots already had lost that game, for all intents and purposes, two weeks earlier in Miami.

"Chuck was such a strong, dominant leader," Nelson said. "We had such faith in him. We depended on him. The announcement that he was leaving was shocking and demoralizing. It totally knocked the team for a loop."

The Oilers won easily 31–14, and it would be 18 years before the Patriots would play another postseason game on their home field.

"The loss in '76 was more frustrating," Nelson said. "In '76 we had a series of judgment calls go against us. In '78 we lost because of internal problems."

"It seemed," Francis said, "as if, every year, something happened to us."

Bucko

Before there was Bledsoe there was Bucko and his buddy, Bill McPeak.

"We were the first scouting combine," said Bucko Kilroy, thinking back to the days when he and McPeak toured the country in search of prospects.

Later they combined their talents in New England, where Kilroy's astute scouting methods helped Chuck Fairbanks reverse the fortunes of a franchise that had been struggling for a decade. With the Patriots McPeak's specialty was the evaluation of pro personnel.

Both had been outstanding players—Kilroy with the Eagles and McPeak with the Steelers. So they knew what it took to excel in what Kilroy always called "the National League."

Scouting wasn't a full-time proposition when they were pioneers in the field. "We were a couple of weekend commandos," Kilroy said.

Consequently, the draft was a much more haphazard proposition than the highly sophisticated, computerized operation it is today.

"The draft used to be a one-day marathon that lasted from 9:00 AM to 3:00 AM," Kilroy said. "After midnight everybody was kind of groggy. Heck, nobody knew who they were drafting after the first three hours anyway.

"So, to liven things up, somebody would draft a comic-strip character. You know, a guy would stand up and say, 'Such and such a team drafts Joe Palooka.' That would make [NFL commissioner] Bert Bell mad. He'd holler at the guys to quit fooling around, to get serious. But they may as well have drafted Joe Palooka. They didn't know who they were getting anyway." When McPeak became head coach of the Redskins in 1961, the team had no organized system of evaluating talent.

"The owner, George Preston Marshall, thought it was too expensive," he said. "After my first year, when we went 1–12–1, I explained to him how a lack of scouting was really costing us.

"I asked him to let me scout just the Southeastern Conference and the Atlantic Coast Conference. I told him I'd be gone six weeks. Then he could look at the expense account and, if he thought he could live with it, we should do it on a national level.

"He let me go, and I stayed in the cheapest motels and I ate in cafeterias. When I got back and he saw what I had done, he was angry with me. He said, 'Don't stay in places like that when you're representing the Washington Redskins. Stay in good places. Eat in decent restaurants.'"

Marshall was not displeased with the reception McPeak's efforts received from the local media.

"He was always publicity conscious, and he was very impressed that the press was interested and receptive," McPeak said. "That was the beginning of the scouting program in Washington."

Kilroy made his reputation as a superscout with the Cowboys in the mid-1960s. He came to New England from Dallas in 1971 and revamped and revitalized the Patriots' scouting department.

With Kilroy calling the shots, the Patriots, who didn't have a winning season from 1967 until 1976, drafted the likes of John Hannah and Mike Haynes—both future Hall of Famers—Steve Grogan, Stanley Morgan, Pete Brock, Steve Nelson, Ray Clayborn, Sam Cunningham, Andy Johnson, Julius Adams, Tim Fox, and Russ Francis—turning the team from a perennial also-ran into a perennial playoff contender.

In 1975 the Cowboys were hoping to draft Francis, figuring people wouldn't know about the talented tight end from Oregon because he had chosen not to play as a senior.

But coach Tom Landry told Gil Brandt, who was the personnel director in Dallas, "If he's what you say he is, he'll never get by Bucko."

Very little got past Kilroy—including, in his playing days, ball carriers. He played 13 seasons for his hometown Philadelphia Eagles and was voted All-Pro in six of them—three times on offense as a guard from 1948 to 1950, and then three times on defense as a middle guard from 1952 to 1954.

Big at 6'2" and 250 pounds, tough, and durable, he didn't miss a game from 1947 through 1954 and helped the Eagles win championships in 1948 and 1949.

"I enjoyed playing defense," he said. "Offense was drudgery. Defense was fun."

Al "Dee-Ro" DeRogatis, a lineman for the New York Giants and later a network-television analyst, claimed that, back in the days when players didn't wear face masks, Kilroy bit him on the nose.

Kilroy was offended that Dee-Ro would say such a thing. "I never bit him on the nose," Kilroy insisted. "I bit his ear."

Kilroy always enjoyed relating such stories, often doing so using phrases that writers who covered the Patriots referred to as "Bucko-isms."

When, for example, Kilroy thought something was too expensive, he said it was "cost-prohibited." In the middle of heated negotiations with Howard Slusher, the agent for John Hannah and Leon Gray, who was concerned about collusion among league owners when the two All-Pro offensive linemen were holding out in 1977, Bucko declared in exasperation, "Howard's accusing me of collision."

Names sometimes were a problem for Kilroy. He referred to Napoleon McCallum, a standout running back at Navy, as "that Bonaparte kid." Unable to differentiate between Mike Madden, who covered the Patriots for the *Boston Globe*, and Kevin Mannix, the beat man for the *Boston Herald*, Kilroy called both of them "Maddux."

Then there was the time a couple of writers were sitting with Kilroy and Patriots coach Ron Meyer poolside at a hotel in Palo Alto, near Stanford University, where the team was training between a couple of preseason games in California. The subject under discussion was the Fellowship of Christian Athletes and how the organization had grown and spread throughout the NFL.

The look on Meyer's face was unforgettable when Kilroy began to chortle his distinctive "Heh-heh-heh!" and said, "We invented Christianity back in Philadelphia in the '40s." It took a while before Meyer understood that Kilroy was talking about an early FCA group.

Back in the days when NFL players had jobs in the off-season, Kilroy was employed by Madison Square Garden, where one of his responsibilities was the supervision of the maintenance, assembling, and transportation of a banked wooden running track that was shipped all over the country for meets.

He once took it across the country to Pasadena, where more than 60,000 people turned out for a meet at the Rose Bowl. Among those in attendance was an athletics promoter from South America who inquired about purchasing the track.

"We negotiated for while," Kilroy said, "and he bought it. I had to get all the pieces of the track from Pasadena to the port of Los Angeles. We got it stowed on board a freighter, and I got the check in my hand before they sailed away. Good thing, too, because we got word that the ship sank halfway to Purdue."

When it came to evaluating prospects, though, Kilroy made few misstatements or mistakes. "I had a theory of how to measure players' athletic ability," he said. "The more measurements you got, the more you could confirm. Anything else was an estimate, an opinion. I'd refine the system every year."

Russ Francis

Howard Cosell called him "All-World," which, while highly complimentary, wasn't entirely appreciated by Russ Francis, the highly talented and even more free-spirited tight end for the Patriots.

"I'm lucky I lived through that," Francis said. "It seemed as if every player that heard that took a personal interest in putting me out of the game. They wanted to prove that I wasn't All-World and that they were. I used to think about thanking Howard while I was sitting in the ice tub after games."

Russ Francis charges ahead for yardage as the Colts' Derrel Luce has a tough time bringing him down in second-period action of this September 12, 1976, game. Photo courtesy of AP Images.

More accurate was Bucko Kilroy's nickname for him, "Kid Charisma." Standing 6'5" and weighing a sculpted 245 pounds, Francis had darkly handsome good looks, similar to those of movie actors Burt Reynolds and Tom Selleck, and was a great natural athlete.

While in high school, he set a national schoolboy record in the javelin throw. He also was drafted as a pitcher by the Kansas City Royals.

He accepted a football scholarship to Oregon but didn't play his senior year because his coach had been fired.

"The coach was Dick Enright. The players really liked him," Francis said. "We thought we were ready to go somewhere with him, but we lost the last game of my junior year to Oregon State, and he was fired. There wasn't much of a relationship between the athletic department and the players. It wouldn't have been any fun to go back and play under those conditions."

And so, even though he had been All-Conference as a junior, Francis sat out his senior season.

"It was my form of protest over the firing," he said. "Some scouts told me I wouldn't be able to play in the NFL because of that. They told me I probably wouldn't get drafted. I remember thinking, *If I don't, I'll do something else.*"

Francis always had a wide variety of interests. He enjoyed skydiving, motorcycle riding, and scuba diving. He also enjoyed flying—particularly an open-cockpit, single-engine Steadman. He also acquired a World War II–vintage P-51 Mustang.

A classic Francis story involves the plane ride over Hawaii he gave Raiders linebacker Phil Villapiano. In the playoff game in Oakland in 1976, Villapiano had all but tackled Francis on a crucial third down but was never penalized. Years later, having volunteered to give Villapiano an aerial tour of the islands, Francis flipped the plane upside down and wouldn't turn it over again until Villapiano admitted he had held him, and then apologized.

That actually was one of Francis' more mild escapades. There was, for instance, the time at the Pro Bowl when he dove from a sixth-floor balcony into the hotel pool.

"It was [Steelers linebacker] Jack Lambert's idea. We were talking about diving off the cliffs in Hawaii into the ocean. I went over to the elevator and pushed number six. I dove, and when I hit the water, I scraped my knees on the bottom. Sometimes I wonder why I did those things."

One night at a going-away party at a Foxboro restaurant for linebacker Steve Zabel, who had a reputation as a wild man, Steve Nelson rammed Francis' head through a wall.

"We were having a good time wrestling," said Francis. "I body-slammed him, and he eye-gouged me. I went to tackle him, and he ducked, and I went into the wall headfirst.

"When I came back the next day to pay for the damage, the owner had had the hole framed. He said he wanted to keep it that way for posterity."

As colorful as his off-field exploits were, Francis earned his place in Patriots lore with his play. Kilroy drafted him in the first round in 1975, 16th overall, and Francis went on to become a three-time Pro Bowl selection.

"He came into the NFL as a freak of nature," said Raymond Berry. "It's unusual to combine the quickness and strength he had. He had great speed, great size—he could do it all. I wouldn't hesitate to call him the most gifted tight end I've ever laid eyes on."

Hannah

How good was John Hannah? He was "The Best Offensive Lineman of All-Time." That, at least, was the headline on the cover of *Sports Illustrated* the week of August 3, 1981.

It was true then—although there are older fans who would argue for Jim Parker, the great tackle on the Baltimore Colts' championship teams of the late 1950s—and it remains true today.

"He was built to be a guard," said Pete Brock, who played center for the Patriots from 1976 through 1987. "With his strength, physique, and passion for the game, he was the best offensive lineman I've ever seen."

Hannah was, indeed, something to see—especially when he pulled his powerful 6'3", 275-pound body out of the line to lead a sweep, his eyes narrowed to slits, his face beet-red, his breath coming in snorts, like an angry bull's charging a matador in the ring.

"John has size, explosiveness, and speed," the late Bucko Kilroy, who drafted him in the first round out of Alabama in 1973 as the fourth choice overall, said of Hannah. "Even more than all of that, he has phenomenal—repeat, phenomenal—lateral agility and balance, like a defensive back. He's a guy capable of positively annihilating an opponent." And he often did.

John Hannah gets some air during the AFC Divisional Playoff Game against the Raiders on January 5, 1986. The Patriots beat the Raiders 27–20 at the Los Angeles Memorial Coliseum.

"You'd see people taking a dive to get out of his way," said Ron Erhardt, who was offensive coordinator for Chuck Fairbanks in 1978, when the Patriots set an NFL record that still stands by rushing for 3,165 yards on 671 attempts.

Erhardt, who succeeded Fairbanks as head coach in 1979 and held the job for three seasons, went on to say, "You'd see John clear out a cornerback, then a safety, and he'd just keep on going. He wouldn't leave his feet. Sometimes he'd just stick out a big paw and swat people out of the way."

John Madden enjoyed watching Hannah more from the television booth than he did when he had to coach against him on the sideline with the Raiders.

"The thing I always liked about Hannah," said Madden, "is that he had a defensive player's attitude—that same aggression."

"He was the most intense player I've ever been around," Patriots quarterback Steve Grogan said. "Not just in games but in practice too—nobody had more intensity than John.

"He never talked to me on game day. My first couple of years, I thought he hated me. Then I found out he stopped talking to his family on Friday night. He wouldn't talk to anyone on Saturday except the other offensive linemen. On Sunday he wouldn't talk to anybody. He was so focused, it was scary."

Yet part of Hannah's motivation, Grogan felt, was based on fear. Not fear of his opponent, certainly, but fear of failure.

"He had a fear of failure," Grogan said. "He simply refused to fail."

Hannah didn't disagree. "There was a certain amount of fear I took into the games," he acknowledged. "Not physical fear, but the fear of being humiliated, being made to look bad."

There weren't many—if any—defensive linemen who could do that. What was more likely was that he would intimidate them.

"He wore the smallest helmet he could squeeze on to his head," Brock said "His face would be all squished up, his eyes would narrow, and the veins would start popping out on his neck."

Then he'd go looking for somebody to hit.

"I remember one time we were playing at Seattle," Brock said. "The Seahawks played a 3-4 defensive front, and they had a linebacker named

Michael Jackson, who used to hang a towel from his waist that hung almost to the ground. Jackson was a finesse player. He relied on speed rather than power.

"Because Seattle played a 3-4, John would come flying out of his stance at Jackson. But instead of taking on the block, Jackson would 'Ole!' him, stepping aside to avoid contact. Jackson wasn't making any tackles, but John wasn't able to get a good lick on him.

"After a quarter and a half, John was frustrated and furious. He turned to me in the huddle and said, 'That S.O.B. won't let me hit him.' To John, that wasn't courageous. That wasn't how you were supposed to play the game."

Hannah played the game as it was meant to be played.

"I don't think any player in the game has ever mastered his position the way John has," said Ron Wooten, who played right guard on the Patriots' 1985 AFC championship team. It was following that Super Bowl that Hannah retired after 13 seasons in New England.

"John Hannah combined extraordinary physical ability with an inner drive to be the very best he can be," said Raymond Berry, who, like Hannah, is a member of the Pro Football Hall of Fame and was coach of that 1985 Super Bowl squad.

"His spirit, intensity, effort, will to win, and competitive nature inspired everyone who played with him—and against him," Berry said. "As a coach, you never have to grade John, because you know what he is doing in every game—playing his guts out."

It's been more than 20 years since Hannah stopped playing, but he still misses the game.

"The greatest time in my life was being in that locker room," he said. "I've never been able to find anything to replace it. I wish I could do it all over again. I'd do it in a heartbeat."

Darryl

What rates as the greatest day in Patriots history could be debated. But there is no question what day is the saddest—August 12, 1978. That was the day wide receiver Darryl Stingley suffered the injury that left him a quadriplegic.

In one horrifying, life-altering split-second a hit by Raiders safety Jack Tatum turned Stingley from a fleet, graceful athlete to a man

Wide receiver Darryl Stingley lies motionless on the field after colliding with the Raiders' Jack Tatum at Oakland Coliseum on August 12, 1978. The collision left Stingley permanently paralyzed. Photo courtesy of AP Images.

confined to a wheelchair for the rest of his life, which came to an end in 2007, at the age of 55.

There was only 1:29 left to play in the first half of the second game of the Patriots' preseason schedule. The Pats were leading 14–7 and faced a second-and-13 situation at the Oakland 24. Stingley was the primary receiver on a play designed to have him slant in over the middle from the right side of the formation.

The pass from Steve Grogan was high, and Stingley had to leap into the air to catch it. As he came down with the ball, he could see Tatum, who had earned a reputation as a vicious hitter, coming toward him at top speed. Instinctively Stingley ducked his head. It was the worst thing he could have done.

The force of the collision was frightening and could be heard throughout the stadium. Tatum drove his shoulder into the top of Stingley's helmet and then hit him with his forearm. As if shot, Stingley fell to the ground and lay motionless.

Tight end Russ Francis ran to him and stood over him. John Hannah, enraged by what he perceived to be an unnecessary cheap shot—especially in a preseason game—had to be restrained from going after Tatum. Clearly Stingley was seriously hurt.

Taken to a nearby hospital, Stingley was found to have a damaged spinal cord. He was almost completely paralyzed. For several weeks his life was in danger; following surgery to realign the dislocation—his C-4 vertebrae had fractured and slipped down over the one below it—he developed pneumonia from a collapsed lung.

He recovered but then faced the daunting, depressing problem of how he would deal with having been transformed from a gifted professional athlete into someone who could hardly move.

"I have relived that moment over and over again," he said in an interview with the Associated Press in 1988. "I was 26 years old at the time, and I remember thinking, *What's going to happen to me? If I live, what am I going to be like?* And then there were all those whys, whys, whys. It was only after I stopped asking why that I was able to go on with my life."

And go on he did. Stingley eventually gained enough movement on his right side that he was able to operate his motorized wheelchair on his own. He often visited paralyzed patients in hospitals and created a foundation to aid inner-city youths in his hometown of Chicago. At the age of 40 he completed requirements for his degree from Purdue, where he'd been such a standout that the Patriots picked him in the first round, 19th overall, in 1973.

Although John Madden, the Raiders' coach, was an almost-daily visitor during the weeks Stingley was hospitalized in Oakland, Tatum never came. Nor, as the months and years rolled by, did he ever contact the man he had put into a wheelchair.

Instead of being angry, Stingley handled the situation with class. "For me to go on and adapt to a new way of life, I had to forgive him," he said. "I couldn't be productive if my mind was clouded by revenge or animosity. I don't harbor any ill feelings toward him. I forgave Jack Tatum a long time ago."

Snow Plow Game

Hanging from the ceiling on the second floor of the Patriots Hall of Fame, that treasure trove of team lore and memorabilia located just outside Gillette Stadium, is a John Deere tractor. If Don Shula had his way, Ron Meyer would be hanging right up there alongside it. That tractor is famous to Patriots fans, infamous to Dolphins fans. Patriots fans look up at it and smile. Dolphins fans look at the dark green machine and see red. And it's all because of what took place on a never-to-be-forgotten snowy Sunday in December 1982.

On that day, a young man named Mark Henderson was using that tractor, with a plow attached to the front, to clear the yardage lines at what then was known as Schaefer Stadium.

He'd been doing it throughout the day as the Patriots and Dolphins slogged through the snow in a scoreless tie. With winds gusting to 30 miles per hour and the fingers of quarterbacks and receivers feeling like icicles, neither team wanted to put the ball in the air very often. And so the game became a wintry version of "three yards and a cloud of dust"— or, more accurately, two yards and a dusting of snow.

But, thanks largely to the bullish rushes of fullback Mosi Tatupu, who earned the nickname of "the Snowin' Samoan" because of his ability to plow ahead through uncertain footing, the Patriots found themselves in position, with 4:45 remaining, to kick a game-winning field goal.

They'd gotten to the Miami 16-yard line and sent their left-footed kicker, a former soccer player from England named John Smith, on to the field. While Smith didn't have great range, he was very accurate and, under normal conditions, would be expected to make the kick with ease.

But nothing was easy on this day, given the wet, slippery, snowy conditions.

In the second quarter Smith had missed an 18-yard attempt when he slipped approaching the ball and drilled a low line drive off the helmet of one of his offensive linemen.

So with the Patriots having called a timeout to prepare for the kick that in all likelihood would be their last chance to score, Smith was on his knees, scraping at the hard-packed snow, trying desperately to clear a spot. Matt Cavanaugh, his holder and the backup quarterback, was trying to help. Neither took much notice of Henderson, heading toward them on the John Deere, sweeping clear the stripe marking the 20-yard line.

"I was just trying to find a spot to put the ball down," Cavanaugh said. "The next thing I know, the tractor was coming up behind me. He must have seen me mark off a spot before the timeout, because he drove right over the middle of where I was going to put the ball down."

Shula was incensed, but what could the officials do, push the snow back over the suddenly green spot on the artificial turf?

When Smith, able to step firmly toward the ball, planted his right foot, pivoted, and swung through with his left, kicking the ball squarely through the uprights, Shula was so hot it was surprising the snow didn't melt along the Miami sideline.

A large part of the reason he was so irate was that during the timeout he had seen Patriots coach Ron Meyer run along the opposite sideline, waving Henderson on to the field and pointing toward the spot where Smith wanted to kick.

"This is the last thing you'd want to see in pro football," the steaming Shula said after the game. "The officials never should have let it happen."

But the officials didn't realize what was happening until it was too late.

"The game officials had no control over something like that," referee Bob Frederic explained. "At the time the sweeper came out, it was not under our control or jurisdiction." Frederic went on to add that if the Dolphins had moved into field-goal range in the final minutes, he would have insisted that Henderson clear a spot for them to kick, too. "We very clearly told coach Shula that we would also have swept their area," he said.

What Shula wanted to do was wipe his locker room floor with Meyer. "The thing that disturbs me most," said Shula, "is his taking pride in what he did."

At first Meyer tried to deny he'd done anything at all. He attempted to feign innocence, insisting he was as shocked as anyone when Henderson swerved to plow a place for Smith to kick.

When it was pointed out to him that he had been seen waving at Henderson, Meyer replied, "I was just waving at the kicker to kick it through."

That was typical of Meyer, who had come to New England after a highly successful stint at Southern Methodist, where, the joke went, his payroll was higher than Billy Sullivan's was with the Patriots.

"When we were interviewing him," Pat Sullivan said, "there was a lot of talk about SMU receiving the 'death penalty' from the NCAA for infractions that occurred when Ron was coaching there.

"Now, we really didn't care about that. But we did want to know what the story was, so we asked him if he had given any of the players money."

According to Sullivan, Meyer replied, "Quite honestly, we did give [All-American running back] Eric Dickerson some cash. But the poor kid had no money to put gas in the car that Texas A&M had bought him."

That was classic Meyer.

As they say in Texas, he was "all hat and no cattle." Which is to say he had more style than substance. His success as a college coach was primarily due to recruiting. In the NFL he had to do some serious coaching, and he wasn't up to the task.

He got off on the wrong foot with Hall of Fame guard John Hannah when he insisted before the Pats' first preseason game—against the Steelers in Knoxville, Tennessee—that all the offensive players ride on one bus and the defensive players on another. To Hannah it smacked of high school, as did much of the rest of the way Meyer acted.

"He knew nothing about football," Hannah said disdainfully.

After insisting he knew nothing about what Henderson did with the snow plow, Meyer finally fessed up. "I waved him on," he acknowledged. "I wanted him to brush off the snow. I was unaware of any illegal aspects. To me, it was just a spur-of-the-moment decision. There wasn't anything malicious about it. I saw John on his hands and knees trying to get the snow cleared and, all of a sudden, it hit me. Why not send a plow out there?

"I kept looking for it, but I had trouble finding it. I was about to forget about the whole thing when I saw [Henderson], so I ran down and told him to plow the spot John was trying to clear."

What makes the story even more amusing was Henderson was a convict, serving a 15-year sentence for burglary, who was on work release from a nearby prison.

"Afterwards," Pat Sullivan said, "I told Henderson to avoid the press. Of course, he didn't. There was a guy from the *Miami Herald* who was as angry about the whole thing as Shula. He was practically shouting at Henderson, saying, 'Do you know that Coach Shula is on the NFL Competition Committee? Do you know how well respected he is around the league? Do you know what the penalties for this could be?' Henderson just smiled at him and said, 'What are they going to do? Throw me in jail?'"

Sullivan still laughs at the memory. "The writer had no clue," he chuckled, "that Henderson was out on a work-release program."

chapter 5

Billy Sullivan

To begin to understand and appreciate Billy Sullivan, you first have to understand what a Kernwood is.

Sullivan loved to play golf. He loved to wager on golf. The negotiations on the first tee at Oyster Harbors, near his home in Cotuit on the south shore of Cape Cod, were as spirited as any he ever had with John Hannah, Leon Gray, or Mike Haynes over a contract.

Sullivan's favorite wager was a convoluted bit of financial finagling he called a "Kernwood," in which, on the final hole of the match, the player who was losing made three separate wagers, each for the amount of the original stake. On one bet, he'd receive a full shot from his opponent. On the second, a half shot. The third wager was played even-up.

Since Sullivan's enthusiasm for the game exceeded his ability, he usually was in arrears on the 18th hole and so he would optimistically, but also adamantly, insist on playing a Kernwood. More often than not, he'd rise to the occasion and bail himself out.

But win or lose, it was a delight to listen to him in the clubhouse later, libation in hand, describe how he triumphed over adversity or bemoan the evil fates that cost him victory.

Sullivan had the gift of gab. As a friend once said of him, "You ask Billy for the time, and he'll tell you how to make a watch."

He was as competitive as he was loquacious. He also could be combative and vindictive as well as charming and considerate. He was both irascible and lovable. There was no middle ground with Sullivan. You were either with him or against him—friend or foe—and he had an abundance of both.

From left are Barron Hilton, president of the San Diego Chargers; Tobin Rote of the Chargers; AFL commissioner Joe Foss; Gino Cappelletti of the Patriots; and Billy Sullivan, president of the Patriots. Foss presented Rote with the award for Western Division Player of the Year and Cappelletti with the award for Eastern Division Player of the Year.

He was the patriarch of the Patriots—the man who brought the NFL back to New England and, more importantly, kept it there when it would have been financially rewarding for him to take, or sell, the franchise to other cities desperately seeking a team.

Sullivan had many offers and opportunities to move the Patriots, but he was a New Englander through and through and that's where he was determined to keep his football team. It was determination that enabled him to land a franchise in the first place.

In the fall of 1959 Bill and his wife, Mary, had saved $8,000 to use as a down payment on a summer house on the Cape. Instead he used it as a down payment on a professional football team.

With that, Sullivan joined seven other men to form the fledgling American Football League. They called themselves "the Foolish Club," and Sullivan may have been the most foolish of them all.

"I was the only man who was not independently wealthy," he liked to say, adding, with his Irish eyes sparkling, "or even dependently wealthy. At the time," he said, "I had $8,000 to my name. I hustled around to come up with the $25,000 the league required." That was pocket money for other owners.

While Sullivan was president of Metropolitan Petroleum Company of Boston, which sold fuel oil, men like Lamar Hunt of the Dallas Texans and Houston's Bud Adams owned oil wells. Sullivan was hoping to buy a house on the Cape. Chargers owner Barron Hilton owned hotels all over the world.

For those owners with family fortunes, a pro football team was a rich man's toy. For Sullivan, it became the family business. His oldest son, Chuck, a lawyer, became executive vice president of the Patriots. His youngest son, Patrick, worked his way up from ball boy to general manager. Another son, Billy, served as director of stadium operations. Daughter Jeanne was on the board of directors. Daughter Nancy did the interior decorating for the stadium offices. His cousin Mary was treasurer, and his cousin Walter was a director. It got so the management page of the Patriots media guide looked like a Sullivan family photo album.

"I have my whole family—my whole life—tied up in the team," Billy said. What he didn't have was enough money. Not really. Not ever.

"It shows how desperate we were," Hunt said, "to take a man with no money and no stadium."

It was Frank Leahy who proved instrumental in helping Sullivan obtain an AFL franchise. Sullivan had been a sports fan all his life. Growing up in the industrial town of Lowell, where his father was a newspaperman, he worked as a stringer for the *Lowell Courier-Citizen* and also served as official scorer, at 50 cents a game, for Lowell Tri-League baseball games in order to earn tuition money at Boston College. He graduated from Boston College in 1937 and a year later convinced his alma mater to hire him as its first director of publicity.

Leahy's image was a shadow of what it would become when he was lured away from Fordham to coach the Boston College football team.

Notre Dame coach Frank Leahy uses a microphone to direct his players during practice in September 1947.

"I remember so well the headline when [Leahy] left Fordham to begin his incredible success story at Boston College," Sullivan wrote in the foreword to *Shake Down the Thunder*, a Leahy biography written by Wells Twombly. "The words screamed forth, 'Unknown Leahy Signed by Boston College.' When I met him, he looked at me and said, 'How do you do? I am Unknown Leahy.'"

He wasn't unknown for long. He took the Eagles to the Cotton Bowl in 1939, only his second season on the job, and then led them to the Sugar Bowl the following year when, led by All-American Charley O'Rourke, Boston College went undefeated, capping the season by beating Tennessee.

Leahy had been a standout lineman for Knute Rockne at Notre Dame, which hired him to coach the Fighting Irish in 1941 after his success at Boston College. Impressed with Sullivan's publicity work and enjoying his conviviality, Leahy brought Billy with him to South Bend, where he was the "ghost writer" for a nationally syndicated newspaper column published under Leahy's name.

Both men entered the navy during World War II, with Sullivan continuing his public-relations work at the Naval Academy in Annapolis. When the war ended Sullivan went back to Boston, where he landed a job as publicity director for the Boston Braves of the National League. In that capacity he helped found the Jimmy Fund, which raises money for research and treatment of cancer in children, and also produced the first promotional film ever made for a professional baseball team.

That experience in film led to a joint venture with Leahy, making instructional sports films. But he didn't like working in Los Angeles and commuting cross-country on weekends to see his growing family, which remained behind in Boston.

So in 1955 he decided to come back East and start his own public-relations firm in Boston. One of the companies he hoped to land as a client was Metropolitan. The president of the company was a Boston College man who was nearing retirement and looking for a successor. He convinced Billy to come to work for Metropolitan, and three years later he was running the company.

But what he really wanted to run was a professional sports franchise. He figured it had to be football because he knew the Red Sox would use all their influence to prevent another National League team from coming into the city after the Braves left for Milwaukee in 1953.

He had hoped to obtain an NFL expansion franchise, but that dream died in 1958 along with his friend and ally, league commissioner Bert Bell.

That's when Leahy stepped in. The old coach was working for Barron Hilton in L.A. as general manager of the Chargers and was well aware that an eighth team was required to round out the new league. He contacted Sullivan, who of course was interested, and Leahy then set about convincing people that Sullivan would be a good owner, despite lacking a stadium and funds.

"He never forgot someone who stood at his side," Sullivan wrote of Leahy. "The [AFL] expansion committee consisted of Frank, Harry Wismer of the New York Titans, and Lamar Hunt of the Dallas Texans. I knew Wismer well because he had done the broadcasts of Notre Dame games when I was there working with Frank. But Lamar Hunt didn't know me whatsoever. Many cities were being considered.... At the last moment I got on the telephone and told [Leahy] that I had a group put together that had enough money to make the project a success. There was one major objection—we had no place to play. I was quite worried about that.

"I should have known [Leahy] better than that. I learned later that, out of loyalty to me, he contacted each of the club presidents and per-suaded them that Boston should have a team. Frank Leahy was a most persuasive man."

On November 18, 1959, Sullivan was granted an AFL franchise for Boston. He rounded up nine other investors, each putting up $25,000—one of them was former Red Sox star Dom DiMaggio, brother of Joe—and a decision was made to sell nonvoting stock to the general public to raise more operating capital.

"Boston," Hunt once said, "probably had the most unusual begin-nings of any franchise in history. In fact, I'd call them very improbable, especially from the standpoint of what we do today—all the research that goes into the people, the city, all those kinds of things. But I guess there never would have been an American Football League if we'd had enough sense to do those things.

"I admire [Sullivan] so much for his stick-to-itiveness and the way he's fought, scraped, and clawed, trying to make things go on a shoe-string budget."

Sullivan's lack of funds too often resulted in a lack of quality players, especially in the late 1960s and early 1970s.

"I was a great admirer of Billy's," said Jon Morris, a six-time AFL All-Star center and once an NFL Pro Bowler. "I liked him very much and feel a great deal of loyalty toward him. But the fact is that he always was trying to do it with smoke and mirrors. And because he had no money, we had bad teams. He ran the operation on a shoestring, and the fans paid the price."

Morris remembers that after turning down the Green Bay Packers, who also had drafted him, in order to sign with the Patriots, he didn't get a check the first two paydays his rookie year.

"I felt like I was back at Holy Cross," he said, chuckling because he didn't realize that, because the treasurer of the team at the time also worked for a local bottling company, the game checks were being sent out in envelopes bearing that firm's logo rather than the Patriots'.

"I threw them away, thinking they were junk mail," Morris said.

In 1973 and 1974 Sullivan nearly lost control of the team in a power struggle with other stockholders. There had been some turnover among the original investors, and by that time 34 percent of the voting stock was controlled by two men from New York—David McConnell and Robert Wetenhall. Sullivan owned less than 24 percent. Another 14 percent belonged to Dan Marr Jr. and Bob Marr, who had inherited it from their father, one of the men Sullivan had brought in at the beginning of the franchise.

With the team struggling—they'd suffered through seven straight losing seasons—and finances always tight, neither the Marrs nor the New Yorkers thought Sullivan should continue to run the team.

"The whole franchise was adrift," Bob Marr said. "The team was not doing well. Boston was down on the team, and the sale of season tickets was down. We had to have some changes made."

It appeared as if Sullivan was going to be out as team president in January 1973, but he prevailed upon Hessie Sargent, the widow of his old friend and original investor George, to grant him another year on the job.

Sullivan scrambled to put off the inevitable, trying to convince Mrs. Sargent to sell her stock to him. He already could count on the 12.5 percent owned by his cousin Mary, the daughter of Sullivan's late uncle

Joe Sullivan, from Lowell. Gaining control of the Sargent stock would make him a majority owner, albeit narrowly.

But Mrs. Sargent, on the advice of her son Lee—who was no ally of Sullivan's—refused to sell, and so Sullivan was voted out in April 1974.

He did not go quietly. Popular with his fellow owners, they let it be known they were not happy Old Billy had been forced out. He continued to lobby Mrs. Sargent to sell her stock to him. The difficulty for Sullivan was that he also had to offer to buy the Marrs' stock and that of McConnell and Wetenhall at the same price of $112 per share. Needless to say, he had to borrow that money.

His son Chuck, by then a top attorney with the firm of Edwards & Angell in New York City, arranged the financing, and when the smoke cleared Sullivan owned 88 percent of the team. He had not purchased his cousin Mary's shares, instead promising to do so over the next several years.

Had he sold out himself, Sullivan could have pocketed roughly $3 million. Instead, he wound up nearly $8 million in debt. Which, to put that in perspective, was more than he had spent to build the stadium in Foxboro. He then spent another $3 million to buy out the nonvoting shareholders.

"That shows you how smart I am," he said. "I owned the whole thing for $25,000, and it cost me $11 million to get it back."

"Billy spent every dime he had on the franchise," said Bucko Kilroy. "He had many chances to move the team and pay off all his debts, but he always turned them down."

Among the cities that tried to convince Sullivan to leave Boston, especially when he was having so much trouble getting a stadium built, were Seattle, Memphis, Jacksonville, Tampa, and Birmingham, Alabama. But the man who brought the Patriots to New England was determined to keep them there. And as many debts as he had, Patriots fans owe him a much larger one that never can be repaid.

"Billy Sullivan was the father of professional football in New England," said current Patriots owner Robert Kraft. "Everyone connected with the Patriots, every football fan in New England, owes him a debt of gratitude."

A Close Shave

It was a close shave.

Victor Kiam, who liked his Remington razor so much he bought the company, purchased the Patriots from Billy Sullivan in 1988. He in turn sold the team four years later to James Busch Orthwein, who, it seemed, planned to take the team out of New England and move it to his native St. Louis, which had lost the football Cardinals to Arizona. In the end that was, indeed, a very close shave for Patriots fans.

Sullivan was prompted to sell his beloved Patriots primarily because he was getting on in years and he knew that his heirs never would have been able to pay the estate taxes upon inheriting the team. Factor in that his oldest son, Chuck, had lost an estimated $20 million promoting pop star Michael Jackson's Victory Tour, along with the fact that the team was chronically short of cash, and it was no surprise when Sullivan put the Pats on the market.

"That was a very difficult period in my father's life," Pat Sullivan said.

It wasn't easy for Sullivan to part with the Patriots. What he absolutely couldn't bear was to see the team leave New England. Not after he fought so hard to keep them in the region, spurning numerous financially attractive offers from other cities over the years.

"One of the reasons the team ended up with Kiam," Pat Sullivan said, "was that Victor promised he wouldn't move it. Of course, that promise lasted all of three years."

Those were difficult times for Kiam, too, although many of his problems were of his own making.

As Pat Sullivan noted, Kiam had "made a fortune on Remington. He built a great business." Building a great football team proved beyond Kiam's capability, however.

His first mistake was failing to buy the stadium along with the team. Although the no-frills stadium beside Route 1 cost less than $7 million to build, that was a lot of money for Billy Sullivan in 1970. In order to finance it, Chuck Sullivan created a real-estate investment trust called Stadium Realty Trust.

When Chuck Sullivan became involved in his ill-fated venture with the Victory Tour involving Michael Jackson, the stadium was used as collateral for loans he took out and eventually found he could not repay. The stadium wound up in bankruptcy court to be sold to the highest bidder.

"We told Victor he absolutely had to buy the stadium," Pat Sullivan said. Kiam wasn't averse to the idea, but he wanted to do it on the cheap. He couldn't believe anyone would buy the stadium if they didn't also own the team.

"Kiam wanted to nickel and dime the deal," Pat Sullivan said. "He was offering about $18 million. He had heard rumors of Bob Kraft offering upwards of $20 million but said, 'The guy's a fool to pay that much.'" As it turned out Kiam was the fool, in more ways than one.

Kraft's shrewd purchase of the stadium and the lease with the Patriots that went with it, guaranteeing the club could play nowhere else through the 2001 season unless the team was prepared to pay prohibitively expensive treble damages to break the lease, turned out be a critical move in his quest to buy the franchise. Under Kiam's ownership the Patriots seemed to be diminishing in value daily.

In 1989 the Patriots had their first losing season in eight years, and coach Raymond Berry was fired. He was replaced by Rod Rust, after which the team hit rock bottom in more ways than one.

Not only did they go 1–15 in 1990, which was humiliating enough in itself, but what was worse was the national embarrassment the franchise suffered when several players cavorted in the nude around a young female sportswriter in the locker room while making lewd comments and gestures.

Instead of being apologetic, Kiam was overheard the following week in the team's locker room in Cincinnati referring to the writer, Lisa Olson of the *Boston Herald*, as "a classic bitch."

He later said his remarks were misconstrued but also told the paper's editors they were "asking for trouble by sending a female reporter to cover the team."

When such comments and crass behavior became known across the country, it proved more than a little troublesome for the sale of Lady Remington shaving products.

The team, which had enough problems simply playing the game, had to go through weeks of interviews with league investigators that were disruptive and, for the players, divisive.

"This entire incident was distasteful, unnecessary, and damaging to the league and others. It included a mix of misconduct, insensitivity, misstatements, and other inappropriate actions or inaction, all of which could and should have been avoided," NFL commissioner Paul Tagliabue, who is also a lawyer, wrote to Kiam when the inquiry finally was over.

Yet Kiam didn't seem to learn anything from the travesty his team's travails had become. Speaking at dinner in Connecticut after the season, he made a tasteless joke about Olson and "Patriot missiles."

With his only football-related revenues coming from the league's television contract and plunging ticket sales—Kraft got all the money from concessions and parking—Kiam decided to sell the team. Enter Orthwein who, to his credit, rejuvenated the franchise by luring Bill Parcells out of retirement to coach the team.

He also offered Kraft $75 million, attempting to buy his way out of the lease binding the Patriots to play in Foxboro for another nine years. Kraft could have gotten out then with a healthy profit. But it wasn't money he was seeking; it was ownership of the Patriots.

Unable to take the team to St. Louis, Orthwein sold the Patriots to Kraft in January 1994 for $172 million—a record price at the time for an NFL franchise.

In the fall of 2008 *Forbes* magazine valued the Patriots at $1.3 billion, ranking New England third in the NFL, behind only the Washington Redskins at $1.5 billion and the Dallas Cowboys at $1.6 billion.

"If we hadn't had that stadium lease," Kraft said, "there's a high probability this team would have been in St. Louis."

chapter 6

1985

It's been overshadowed by the Patriots' three Super Bowl victories, but the AFC Championship Game on January 12, 1986 still rates as one of the truly great triumphs in franchise history.

Not only did it make the Patriots the first team in NFL history to reach the Super Bowl by winning three playoff games on the road, but it also snapped their embarrassing, long-running 18-game losing streak in the Orange Bowl.

Quarterback Steve Grogan said there was even more than that to the upset of the Dolphins, who had been to the Super Bowl the year before and haven't been back since.

"That was the first time I think people in New England really appreciated professional football," he said. "I remember driving to the airport and seeing people pulling over to the side of the road honking their horns and waving as our bus went past. That was the first time football was really special around here."

Before that the Patriots had by and large been fourth among the region's major professional sports team in both affection and attention, ranking behind New England's first love, the Red Sox; the Celtics, who had all those NBA championship banners hanging from the ceiling of the venerable Boston Garden; and even the NHL Bruins, who had been No. 1 when Bobby Orr, Phil Esposito, and company were bringing the Stanley Cup to Boston.

With that win over Don Shula's Dolphins in Miami in the AFC Championship Game, the team so often referred to as "the Patsies" truly became the Patriots. Rather than a source of humor—or humiliation—they had become a source of pride.

Certainly the 1985 team could be proud of its historic march through the playoffs, which began at the Meadowlands against the Jets; moved to the West Coast, where they came from behind to beat the Raiders in Los Angeles; then switched to south Florida, where Dan Marino was throwing touchdown passes in Miami the way revelers throw beads during Mardi Gras in New Orleans.

What Waterloo was to Napoleon, what Watergate was to Nixon, the Orange Bowl was to the Patriots. The Pats went to Miami every year to play their AFC East rivals. And every year for 18 years they lost—including a tough 30–27 setback in a Monday night game in December, only a month earlier. To get back there in the playoffs and try to break that streak would be no easy task.

To begin with, the Patriots never had won a postseason NFL game. And they would have to win two games on two different coasts to have another chance at beating the defending conference champion Dolphins.

First up were the Jets at the Meadowlands. They went down 26–14 as the Patriots forced four turnovers, including a fumble that linebacker Johnny Rembert returned 15 yards for a touchdown. Rookie defensive end Garin Veris had three sacks and an interception. Tony Eason threw a 36-yard touchdown pass to Stanley Morgan, barefooted kicker Tony Franklin booted four field goals, and the Patriots had their first NFL playoff victory.

So it was off to Los Angeles to play the Raiders in the Coliseum, where the Pats fell behind 17–7 six minutes into the second quarter.

"Our guys were saying, 'They have to throw the ball now,'" said Mike Haynes, the Hall of Fame cornerback who played in New England from 1976 through 1982 before going to the Raiders. "I said I didn't think so."

Haynes had been with the Patriots when they set an NFL rushing record in 1978. The 1985 team didn't run the ball that well, but they still had John Hannah, one of the greatest linemen in NFL history, at left guard and preferred keeping the ball on the ground to putting it in the air.

Using mostly running plays, New England took the ensuing kickoff after Marcus Allen's touchdown run had put the Raiders up by 10 points and pounded 80 yards in 10 plays, Craig James following Hannah around left end for the touchdown.

The New England Patriots defense signals that they've recovered a fumble against the Miami Dolphins in the 1985 AFC Championship Game on January 12, 1986.

"They kept their composure," Haynes said. "They kept the ball on the ground. They made some big runs in that drive. They didn't panic. That's what championship teams are made of."

The Patriots continued to run the ball, maintaining possession for 36:59 on their way to a 27–20 come-from-behind victory over the Raiders that earned them a return trip to Miami.

The winning touchdown was scored in the third quarter, when rookie defensive back Jim Bowman fell on a fumbled kickoff in the end zone.

Despite their lengthy losing streak in the Orange Bowl, the Patriots went to Miami confident they could win. They were sure they could run the ball against the Dolphins, who ranked 23rd in the league in rushing defense and had given up 251 yards on the ground in their 24–21 conference semifinal win over the Browns the week before.

"We matched up well with them," New England linebacker Steve Nelson said. "We knew they'd have a hard time stopping us from running the ball and that they'd have a hard time throwing against us."

The defensive key for the Patriots, said Nelson, was cornerback Raymond Clayborn. "Clayborn could match up with their two great receivers, Mark Duper and Mark Clayton. We left him in man coverage against whichever receiver they sent to his side and pushed all the help to Ronnie Lippett, the cornerback on the other side.

"Raymond was unbelievable that day," Nelson said. "He shut down everyone he was up against. I don't think anybody caught a ball on that side of the field all day."

Despite their confidence in Clayborn, the Patriots didn't want to give Marino—who'd set an NFL record the previous year by throwing 48 touchdown passes—too many chances. So, as they had against the Raiders, the Patriots were determined to run the ball and control the clock, which is exactly what they did.

The Patriots ran for 255 yards and racked up an overwhelming advantage in time of possession, 39:51 to 20:09. James ran for 105 yards on 22 carries. Robert Weathers added 87 on 16 carries, and Tony Collins gained 61 yards on 12 attempts.

"Our offensive line was blowing 'em off the ball," Collins said. "We felt like we could run inside, outside, anywhere we wanted."

"Our game plan," said Weathers, "was to use as much of the clock as we could to keep Marino off the field. Our offensive line was very aggressive. They wanted to go right at those guys."

The Patriots didn't have to go to the air very often. Eason threw just 12 times and completed 10—three of them short passes for touchdowns.

When the Dolphins did get their hands on the ball, they quickly coughed it up, losing four fumbles and having two passes intercepted.

"Every time we turned it over," Marino said, "it seemed like they scored. That's why they're going to the Super Bowl."

What should have been the Patriots' finest hour—Super Bowl XX—turned into their longest day.

Unable to control Chicago's overwhelming, overpowering defense, the Patriots were trounced 46–10 by the Bears, at the time the most one-sided Super Bowl in history.

"The Bears constantly attacked," Grogan said. "They brought pressure like I'd never seen. They were totally dominating. It was hard just to make a first down against them, never mind a touchdown."

Grogan and Eason

Steve Grogan had the lanky build and poker face of a Western gun-fighter. Think Gary Cooper in *High Noon*. Quiet but tough.

As for Tony Eason, well, as he put it, "In the minds of a lot of people, I'm the guy from California who wears flip-flops and is laid back."

Unfortunately what sticks in the minds of too many Patriots fans is the damning statement made by all-time All-Pro guard John Hannah that Eason should have played wearing a skirt. By saying that, Hannah stuck a very good player with a very bad rap, as Raymond Berry—who coached Hannah, Eason, and Grogan—attests.

"Anyone who says Tony Eason wasn't tough, that he wasn't a leader, that he didn't have a good arm, is ignorant of the facts," Berry said.

Among the facts many fans choose to ignore is that, in 1986, the Patriots finished last in the league in rushing, averaging less than 86 yards a game. But they finished first in the AFC East, largely because Eason completed nearly 62 percent of his passes (276 of 448) and threw for 19 touchdowns with just 10 interceptions—all without the threat of a reliable running game.

Even with rushers, unconcerned about New England's ineffective running attack teeing off on him, Eason still managed to hang in the pocket and complete a high percentage of passes while throwing almost twice as many touchdowns as interceptions.

The year before, when the Patriots were running the ball very well, Eason quarterbacked the first three—and for the team's first 26 NFL seasons, their only—playoff victories, taking them to their first Super Bowl.

Even Grogan, who in 1984 lost the starting job he'd held since 1975 to Eason, says, "Tony was a good kid. We got along well. He had a lot of talent. People just don't appreciate him."

What they didn't appreciate was that, while Grogan would take a helmet in the chest in order to throw the ball downfield, Eason would take a sack rather than put the ball up for grabs. While some of Grogan's gambles paid off, others were intercepted. But fans still preferred his gutsy style to Eason's conservative approach.

"Tony was totally opposite of Steve," said Pats linebacker Steve Nelson.

The tough, hard-nosed Hannah not surprisingly preferred the way Grogan played the game. "Steve would stand in the pocket, hold the ball, know he'd take a lick, and throw. There aren't many quarterbacks who'll do that," Hannah said. "Eason had a good arm, but he didn't want to get hit."

Grogan paid a price for taking so many hits. He had five knee operations, elbow surgery, and a broken leg. He shrugs off such "minor" injuries as separated shoulders, broken fingers, cracked ribs, and concussions. Not as easy to shrug off was a surgical procedure to fuse a disk in his neck. By the end of his career, he was playing with a "horse collar" around his neck and braces on both knees.

That Grogan would hang on to the ball as long as he did in hopes of finding an open receiver, knowing he would absorb such punishment, was two parts heart and one part arm strength. Eason didn't have a cannon for an arm. Accuracy was his biggest asset. When he went deep he'd loft the ball up early and let fleet wideout Stanley Morgan run under it rather than firing it to him on a line. And so, when Eason didn't see any openings in the secondary, he'd go to the ground and take a sack rather than going downfield and risking an interception.

"Steve was much more aggressive," Eason said. "He was more of a riverboat gambler type of guy. He really rolled the dice. My style was more surgeon-like. I liked to pick 'em apart. I wanted to control the clock and not have any turnovers."

A first-round draft pick out of Illinois as part of the great quarterback class of 1983—John Elway, Todd Blackledge, and Jim Kelly were picked ahead of him that year—Eason, drafted 15th overall, was taken before Ken O'Brien and No. 27 Dan Marino. He replaced Grogan as the starter the following year and threw 23 touchdown passes and only eight interceptions while completing more than 60 percent (259 of 431) of his throws—impressive stats for any quarterback, and even more so for one in his first season as a starter.

But Eason struggled at the start of the 1985 season as the Pats stumbled to a 2–3 record, and it was Grogan who came off the bench when Eason was hurt against the Bills and sparked a six-game winning streak that enabled the Patriots to make the playoffs.

Unfortunately Grogan suffered a broken leg in a loss to the Jets. Fortunately Eason was ready to reassume control. It helped that, especially in the playoffs, the Patriots were able to pound the ball at people, enabling Eason to throw when he wanted to rather than when he had to.

In the Pats' three road victories in the AFC playoffs—they were the first wild-card team to reach the Super Bowl by winning three games on the road—Eason had five touchdown passes and didn't throw a single interception.

"Tony was a smart quarterback," wide receiver Cedric Jones said. "He'd rather eat the ball than throw an interception."

Grogan also was a smart quarterback—smart enough to have called his own plays. A fine runner when he first came into the league (his 12 rushing touchdowns in 1976 still is the record for quarterbacks), he made better use of his strong arm as the years went by and his legs absorbed punishment. He just was willing to take more chances than Eason. And more hits.

"I don't gamble in my personal life," he said. "But on the football field I liked to take chances once in a while. I had the good fortune to play for Ron Erhardt and Raymond Berry, who let me call my own plays. That's when I had some of my better years."

Grogan thinks the game would be better if quarterbacks—especially ones as good as Tom Brady—were allowed to do that now.

"The knock against it," said Grogan, "is that the game is more complex now, with more formations, more motion. I don't buy that."

To Grogan, calling the right play was as simple as consulting with his teammates on the field. "When I'd walk into the huddle on first-and-10," he said, "I'd look at John Hannah and Pete Brock and say, 'We need a running play that'll gain four yards. What's gonna go?'

"Or I'd ask Stanley Morgan, 'Can you get the corner?' He might say, 'Not yet. I've got to set him up.' Later in the game he'd tell me, 'It's there now.' Then I'd throw the ball to him, and it usually was a completion."

Grogan continued, "When I'd call a running play, we'd have three or four options of how to block it. The center would make the call. Those guys were smart enough to do that. They don't let the players think for themselves anymore. They utilize their athletic skills but forget about their brains. And I don't know how the quarterbacks can stand the coach talking to them in their helmet."

It sometimes seemed as if Grogan should have played in the days of leather helmets. He was a throwback, a tough guy who would have enjoyed playing both ways, the way Sammy Baugh and Johnny Lujack did.

"The best feeling I ever had," he said, "was in 1985. I hadn't played in about a year. Eason was the starter. But he got hurt against Buffalo in a game in Foxboro. I came off the bench, and we came from behind and won.

"It was the first game my son, Tyler, had been to. I was interviewed for television on the sidelines after the game, and my wife brought him down, lifted him over the wall, and we ran off the field together."

By the time his career was over—his 16 seasons with the Patriots are a club record—Grogan could barely jog, much less run.

He remembers an incident from a game in his latter years involving his good friend and longtime center Pete Brock.

"Pete was playing on two bad knees," Grogan said, "and I was playing on one. I threw a long bomb to somebody, from around our 35 or 40 down to around the 10. I got knocked down just as I threw. Pete came over to help me up and asked, 'Are you okay?'

"I said I was, and he said he was sorry. 'Was that your guy?' I asked him. He nodded, then asked, 'Should we run down there?' I told him there was no rush, that they wouldn't start without us."

In Grogan's early years, the Patriots were a tremendous rushing team, setting a league record in 1978 with 3,165 yards that seems unlikely to ever be broken. But when he did have to throw the ball, his blind side was protected by Hannah and another All-Pro, left tackle Leon Gray.

Gray was traded to Houston prior to the 1979 season in a deal that made Hannah irate and also caused Grogan some concern when a young tackle named Dwight Wheeler took over at left tackle.

After that season—it was the first as head coach for Ron Erhardt—Grogan went to his optometrist for a routine eye exam. The doctor was surprised that Grogan, a right-hander, had a dominant left eye. "If you had the left tackle I had," Grogan deadpanned, "you'd see better out of your left eye, too."

Although Eason and Hannah didn't see eye-to-eye, Eason says he has no regrets about his years with the Patriots and has fond memories of the 1985 season, even though it ended in a 46–10 pounding at the hands of the defensively dominant Bears in Super Bowl XX—a game in which

Eason was pulled in favor of Grogan after failing to complete any of his first six passing attempts and getting sacked three times.

"We couldn't run the ball in '86," he said. "We were much more of a class team in '85. Everybody was really popping at the same time that year. Everybody was in synch. It was a team that had a lot of synergy going for it.

"Looking back at the playoffs, our defense played their butts off, our special teams were awesome—they scored in every game, up to the Super Bowl—and our offense was running effectively and didn't turn the ball over.

"Even though it had been 'forever' since we'd beaten the Dolphins in the Orange Bowl, we had the sense that [the AFC Championship Game] was our game from the get-go. Unfortunately, I think the Bears felt the same way about the Super Bowl."

Eason said he felt good about the Patriots' chances going into that Super Bowl. "I was excited," he said. "I knew it was going to be tough, but I was excited. Then everything spiraled downward so quickly. The wheels came off. We got our butts handed to us on more than just a couple of plays."

Eason's career spiraled downward after he hurt his shoulder in 1987. "I never threw the same after that," he said. "There were some throws I just couldn't attempt."

He wound up being a backup behind Grogan and Doug Flutie in 1988, then Grogan and Marc Wilson in 1989. After a short stint with the Jets, he retired.

"I had a good time in New England," he said. "I know I left there under a cloud. But the more I think back on it, when people ask what it was like for me there, I think about the people I got to play with and the games I got to play in. It was a gas."

Raymond

Russ Francis, the talented tight end who was a three-time All-Pro for the Patriots in the 1970s, tells the best story about Raymond Berry's coaching style.

"Raymond walked up to me before practice one day and—he's about two feet away—tossed me a football, underhand. He doesn't say a word. So I figure he wants to play catch. I toss it back, underhand. Raymond keeps tossing the ball to me, backing up a few feet each time. I just keep tossing it back.

"It's a bizarre scene, you know, because we're not saying a word. Then I notice that every time he catches the ball, he tucks it away. Right side, left side—he'd catch it and tuck it. This goes on for about 10 minutes. Then I catch one and do what he did—tuck it away. He turns without saying a word and walks away. Just like that. Except he's got this grin on his face. All the while, he wanted me to tuck the ball away. It was his way of teaching me how to do it. It's a lesson I've never forgotten."

Patrick Sullivan never forgot the first time he met Berry. "It was 1967, at our first home preseason game. It was played at Harvard Stadium. I was 15 years old and working as an equipment manager. The AFL and NFL had agreed to merge the year before, so this was going to be our first game against an NFL team, and it wasn't just any NFL team; it was the Baltimore Colts. They had players who were legends. Johnny Unitas, Raymond Berry, Lenny Moore. I'm carrying equipment bags and one of the Colts stopped and offered to help. It was Raymond Berry.

"Now, fast-forward to 1978. Chuck Fairbanks had hired Raymond right after the '77 season as an assistant. I was managing the stadium then. It was during the blizzard of '78. I was standing in the lobby of the executive offices and I see a man walking down Route 1. There was no traffic. He was all alone, trudging through the snow toward the stadium. He taps on the glass door and says, 'If you give me a shovel, I'll give you a hand clearing the steps.' It was Raymond. He was living at a motel just down the road."

Berry always was ready to help. So when the Patriots needed someone to calm the troubled waters stirred up by the tempestuous Ron Meyer, Berry was ready to answer the call.

"He's a very religious man," said linebacker Steve Nelson. "He believed there was a reason he'd been called back to the NFL—that it was the place he was meant to be at that time. He felt it was his responsibility to give us his best effort."

As a player or coach, Berry never gave anything less than his best. "My job," he said, after taking over midway through the 1984 season, "is to make something good out of a bad situation."

Patriots head coach Raymond Berry watches the action from the sideline during the Patriots 20–13 victory over the Seattle Seahawks on November 17, 1985 at the Kingdome.

The following year, Berry led the Patriots to what at the time was the best season in their history, winning the AFC championship and getting to the Super Bowl for the first time.

Meyer had come to New England in 1982 to replace Ron Erhardt, who'd been well liked by the players. Management, however, felt Erhardt might have been too easy on the team during a 2–14 season and decided it was time for someone tougher.

Meyer—a flashy man who wore expensive boots, suits, and rings— had been a winner at Southern Methodist, which was Berry's alma mater. But the New England players quickly ascertained that Meyer's success with the Mustangs was due more to recruiting than coaching and that he had more style than substance. So when he came in and cracked down on them, they turned on him. "He was a fraud," said Hall of Fame guard John Hannah, never a man to mince words.

"I made the mistake," Meyer admitted later, "of not communicating as well as I should have. I don't think I was repressive. Change is tough on everybody. I didn't take that into account with the established players." Meyer wanted to make changes that concerned Pat Sullivan, who was general manager at the time.

"He'd come into my office," Sullivan said, "and demand we trade John Hannah, trade Stanley Morgan, trade Tony Collins. He claimed they were dissidents in the locker room. It became a situation where, frankly, we lost confidence in his judgment."

Meyer lost his job when, without discussing the matter with Sullivan, he abruptly fired defensive coordinator Rod Rust.

"You have to discuss the ramifications of something like that," said Sullivan, who proceeded to fire Meyer, bring back Rust, and hire Berry. "We felt we needed a stable situation."

Because Berry had become a legend as a receiver for the Baltimore Colts' championship teams of the late 1950s, the Patriots players immediately respected him. At that time he had been Johnny Unitas' favorite target, and the two combined for 12 receptions for 178 yards and a touchdown in the Colts' 23–17 overtime victory over the Giants in the 1958 NFL title game, considered by many to be the best game in NFL history.

"Playing for him," center Pete Brock said, "you had the feeling that you didn't want to disappoint him. I always felt like I wanted to prove to him that I could have played with him on those great Colts teams."

It also helped that many of the New England veterans had gotten to know Berry when he was an assistant coach under Chuck Fairbanks and then Erhardt in the late 1970s.

"I respected him," quarterback Steve Grogan said, "because, No. 1, he was a Hall of Fame player. And No. 2, we knew the kind of man he was. You could trust him. You could believe what he said." That wasn't the case with Meyer, who often played fast and loose with the truth.

"Coach Berry," said wide receiver Cedric Jones, "emphasized putting the team ahead of yourself—an unselfish type of attitude. We formed a cohesiveness we didn't have before. Guys really cared about each other. When he took over the job, he talked about a family relationship among players as something we would have to have if we were going to be a championship club."

Berry knew what it took to be a champion. He had been meticulous in his preparation as a player, running pass routes over and over until he had the timing down perfectly, and even went so far as to iron his own uniform pants so they'd fit exactly as he wanted. But as a coach he wasn't a micromanager. He treated his players like men, assuming that they had the same goal he did—to win.

The Patriots had lost three of their first five games in 1985 with Tony Eason at quarterback. When Eason got hurt in Game 6 against the Bills in Foxboro, Berry turned to Grogan, who'd been benched by Meyer the previous season.

"Just before I went into the game," Grogan said, "Raymond looked at me and said, 'I think our best chance to succeed is if you call your own plays. Go in there and call your own game.' We came from behind to win that one and went on to win six in a row before I broke a leg against the Jets."

The following year Berry decided to go with the younger Eason over Grogan as the starter. This was in part, he explained to Grogan, because he felt that if he needed to bring someone in off the bench, Grogan would be better in that role.

Even while Grogan was on the sideline, however, Berry had decided the Patriots would be better off if he continued to call the plays. "That kept me involved," Grogan said. "I'd work with the coaches on the game plan each week." The plan worked well, as the Patriots won the division title in 1986.

Sometimes when Berry was standing on the sideline he seemed not so much lost in thought as just plain lost. "People say it's like he's walking around in a daze," said running back Robert Weathers.

Appearances, in Berry's case, were as deceiving as some of the fakes he used to elude defenders during his playing days with the Colts. "He comes across like a Texas hayseed," said Guy Morriss, a veteran offensive lineman who, like Berry, grew up in Texas. "He speaks kind of slow and walks kind of slow, so people think that he thinks kind of slow, too. But it's not that way. His knowledge of the game is incredible."

Just as important was Berry's knowledge of how to handle people.

"I loved that guy," said linebacker Andre Tippett, who joined Berry in the Pro Football Hall of Fame in the summer of 2008. "He understood how to get the most out of everybody."

Pat and Matt

Never fight out of your weight class.

Patrick Sullivan should have thought about that before he became involved in a war of words with Howie Long that led to Sullivan's getting hit in the head by a helmet belonging to Matt Millen.

It was during the AFC divisional playoff between the Patriots and Raiders in the Los Angeles Coliseum in January 1986. There was a long history of bad blood between the two teams, and Long hadn't helped matters by being highly critical of the Patriots organization in the week leading up to the game.

"It seemed," said Sullivan, "as if we'd pick up the paper every day and Howie—who had grown up in Charlestown—was going on about how the Patriots were the most mismanaged team in the league, and if anyone in the organization had half a brain they would have drafted him, and how the game was going to be a huge mismatch.

"During the game, I was standing on our sideline around the 20-yard line, and Dean Brittenham, who was one of our assistant coaches, was riding Howie pretty good. That was out of character for Dean, but I was getting a kick out of it. Howie wasn't. But he thought it was me doing the talking. So he came over toward the sideline and shouted, 'Are you talking to me, you S.O.B.?'

"I said, 'No, I wasn't. But, now that you're here, I'd like to point out that you're getting your ass handed to you. You should do your talking on the field, instead of in the papers.' After the game, as we were celebrating and the Raiders were leaving the field, Howie came over and grabbed me by the arm. I reached for his face mask, and that's when Matt jumped in and smacked me upside the head with his helmet.

"I didn't realize who had hit me until I spun around and saw Millen. I thought to myself, *Uh-oh, that is the single most crazy human being on the field.*"

Fortunately for Sullivan, cooler heads quickly prevailed, and he was taken into the New England locker room to have his head examined.

"One of the writers asked our team doctor, Bert Zarins, how the team had made it through the game medically," Sullivan said. "Dr. Zarins said, 'Outside of our goofy general manager, who needed eight stitches in his head, everybody's okay.'"

In retrospect the situation seems more humorous than dangerous. "We took a red-eye flight back," Sullivan recalled, "and when I arrived home, there was a box on my front porch from the Newton Police Department. It contained a riot helmet and a note that said, 'Please wear this the next time you play the Raiders.'

"Pictures of the tussle ran in papers all over the country. For days, friends were mailing me clippings. There was even one from the *Honolulu Advertiser*. It's funny now, but I'd have to say it was the stupidest thing I ever did."

Fryar

First it was a knife in the kitchen. Then it was a fork in the road. It never came to a spoon up the nose. Not publicly, anyway. Privately—and sometimes not so privately—Irving Fryar partied hard. But he also played hard.

Taken with the first overall pick in the 1984 draft out of Nebraska, the multitalented wide receiver caused trouble for opponents on the football field, even as he always seemed to be getting into trouble off the field.

Where to begin?

There was the incident of the knife in the kitchen when he missed the 1985 AFC Championship Game in Miami because of a wound to his little finger incurred during a domestic dispute with his pregnant wife.

The Patriots won anyway but then were drubbed in the Super Bowl by the Bears, after which Fryar was one of six players identified as having tested positive for drugs during the season.

The case of the fork in the road came up the following season. Upset because he had been injured in a game against the Bills in Foxboro, Fryar left Sullivan Stadium at halftime and jumped into his Mercedes sports coupe. Perhaps considering the sage advice of Yogi Berra, who said, "When you come to a fork in the road, take it," Fryar apparently couldn't make up his mind which way to go and smashed into a tree. He said he wasn't paying attention because he was talking on his car phone.

That incident led to a great line by Jon Morris, the former star center for the Patriots, who was working as the color analyst on the team's radio broadcasts. When Fryar was hurt in another game and play-by-play man Gil Santos announced he was being taken to the locker room, Morris quickly added, "They'd better lock the door."

Trouble seemed to follow Irving the way a cornerback follows a wide receiver. In 1987 he told Boston police he had been robbed outside a jewelry store not far from the city's infamous Combat Zone. In 1988 he was arrested by a New Jersey state trooper who, after stopping Fryar for speeding, discovered he was carrying an array of weapons in the trunk. In 1990 Fryar was arrested in Providence for brandishing a handgun following a fracas at a nightclub in which fellow wide receiver Hart Lee Dykes, the Patriots' first-round pick in 1989, was beaten with a baseball bat. Clearly a film of Fryar's NFL career would more closely resemble *Bonnie and Clyde* than *Rudy*.

Yet, despite all the bad things in which he was involved, Fryar was a good guy. Or at least a likeable guy. And he certainly was talented.

"He's a unique talent," coach Raymond Berry said. "You can do things with him you can't do with other players."

Unfortunately one of the things the Patriots often had difficulty doing was getting Fryar the ball. That was because, by the time he came to New England from Nebraska—where he'd been a consensus All-American and also had been arrested for breaking down the door to his girlfriend's apartment—many of his teammates were far from top performers. Tony Eason had only a few good years left, Steve Grogan was past his prime, and their largely unsuccessful successors—Tommy Hodson, Marc Wilson, Hugh Millen, Tom Ramsey, and Scott Zolak, to name a few—never had a prime.

"He's a very, very talented player," said the late Dick Steinberg, who made a deal with the Bengals to get the first pick overall and draft Fryar. "He's a very emotional, volatile-type personality, but that's one of the things that makes him the player he is. We're hoping maturity will help him harness those emotions in positive ways rather than negative ones."

Eventually it did, as Fryar found religion and became a Pentecostal minister. But that was too late for the Patriots, whose experience with Irving was that they got more than they bargained for from him off the field and not enough on it.

Only twice in his nine years in New England did he lead the team in receptions. The first was in 1990, when he caught 54 passes for 856 yards and four touchdowns, and the Patriots went 1–15. The second was in 1992, when he caught 55 passes for 791 yards and four touchdowns, and the Patriots went 2–14.

The only time he was selected for the Pro Bowl was in 1985, and that was as a punt returner. He ran back two for touchdowns that season and led the league with an average of 14.1 yards on 37 returns.

It tells you all you need to know about the state of the Patriots in those days that, after they traded Fryar to Miami in 1993, where he had Dan Marino to throw him the ball, he made back-to-back Pro Bowls in what were his 10th and 11th seasons in the league. He would go to the Pro Bowl twice more when he was with the Eagles in 1996 and 1997, when he was 34 and 35 years old.

Ah, what he might have done for the Patriots in his prime if only they'd been better able to utilize his multiplicity of talents. And of course, if only he'd been as mature in those days as he became in the latter part of his career.

What he did best in New England was block. There may never have been a better, or more eager, blocker playing wide receiver than Fryar. Standing an even six feet tall, weighing a sculpted 200 pounds, and possessing 4.4 speed in the 40, Fryar enjoyed running into people as much as he did running past them. Part of that may have been that the ball didn't come his way often enough, even when he was open, and so putting a lick on a defender may have been his way of working out some frustration.

"I might catch a ball in the first quarter," Fryar said, "then I might not get another thrown to me until the third quarter."

That wasn't much fun for a guy like Fryar who craved action. He was a young man who enjoyed fast cars and good times. He pulled into training camp one summer at Bryant College in a flashy, new white Corvette with lots of dazzling chrome and a rear spoiler. The diamond studs in his ears flashing like his bright smile, Fryar exclaimed, "Ready to run—just like me! A combination of speed and power." That was Fryar.

"I don't think I'll ever act like an old person," he said, "I want to act young, be a kid, and have fun. You can't let things get you down."

Ironically it wasn't until Fryar began to grow up and act his age that things started looking up for him, both in his personal and his professional lives.

chapter 7

Hall of Famers

The Patriots have had a Hall of Fame since 1991. For years it existed in name only. Then, in the summer of 2008, the Hall at Patriot Place was opened to honor the greatest Patriots of all time and celebrate the team's history.

At the time there were 13 players in the Patriots Hall of Fame, and four of them also are in the Pro Football Hall of Fame in Canton, Ohio.

Here they are, in the order of their election.

John "Hog" Hannah, OG, 1973–1985

When I think of John Hannah, I recall a scene from a long-ago summer at Patriots training camp at Bryant College in Smithfield, Rhode Island.

The offensive linemen were gathered at the far end of one of the practice fields, where a heavy bag hanging on a strong chain was suspended from a metal crossbar between two poles. The linemen were participating in a drill where they would get into a three-point stance, then slam into the bag and block it four or five times. This was taking place in close proximity to a group of fans eagerly watching from behind a wooden hurricane fence.

On the first hit a lineman would give the heavy bag a solid blow, driving it backward. Then it would come swinging back, gathering force and momentum. By the fourth or fifth hit, the tiring lineman wouldn't be blocking the bag as much as he would be fending it off, trying not to let it knock him off balance and send him sprawling in front of the crowd.

Then it was Hannah's turn.

The crowd pushed up against the fence, eager to see the man widely considered the best offensive lineman in NFL history. Hannah, however, was oblivious to them. As he hunkered into his stance, he was totally focused on the bag in front of him. His eyes narrowed. You could see his square jaw clench. His breath was coming in short bursts.

When the whistle blew, Hannah fired out of his stance with astonishing quickness for a man his size (6'3", 275 pounds) and dealt the bag a punishing blow, sending it soaring backward. As it slowly swayed toward him again, Hannah was crouched low, his legs moving like pistons, his powerful hands in front of his chest, his face red.

This time, he sent the bag even higher. Down, down, down it came again and—wham!—up, up, up it went.

Instead of getting tired, Hannah seemed to be just getting into the flow. Sweat was beginning to pour off him, but it was as if he couldn't wait for the bag to come back down. At the same time, there was a split second when the bag seemed suspended at the top of its arc, almost as if it was hesitating, not wanting to dip back to where Hannah was waiting to pound it again.

But that's not what made the scene so memorable.

As Hannah continued to blast the bag, the crowd, which had been pressed up against the fence trying to get as close to the action as possible, began to back away. It wasn't a conscious reaction, but with each ferocious hit the fans shuffled another half-step away, partly in awe, partly as an instinctive gesture of self-preservation, the way you'd step back from a roaring fire.

It also had become eerily quiet. The only sounds were Hannah's locomotive-like breathing, the quick movement of his feet on the grass, and the resounding "Thwump!" as he hit the big bag.

It was only afterward, when the assistant coach grabbed the bag and Hannah stepped away, a smile spreading across his sweaty face, that the crowd exploded in appreciative and admiring cheers and again drew closer.

Hog was the first Patriots player to be inducted into the Pro Football Hall of Fame, in 1991. One of two players named to the NFL's 75th anniversary team—cornerback Mike Haynes was the other—Hannah was selected to play in nine Pro Bowls, a franchise record.

Gino Cappelletti, WR-K, 1960–1970

Cappelletti played 153 games over 11 seasons for the Patriots but doesn't hesitate for a second when asked to recall his best one.

"That's easy. It was the 1964 season. We were 5–2–1 and fighting Buffalo and Houston for the division lead. We were playing the Oilers at Fenway Park and were leading 22–21 with a minute to go. I'd already kicked three field goals. But then George Blanda kicked one for Houston with about 35 seconds left, and they led 24–22. The people in the stands were starting to leave. After we got the ball I caught two passes near the sideline and ran out of bounds each time. With one second left, we had the ball around the Houston 25. Suddenly, where there hadn't been any crowds, people started closing in on the field. I got ready to attempt a field goal, and the Oilers called timeout. When play resumed I made the kick from 42 yards. The ball was in the air when the game ended. It cleared the crossbar and we won 25–24. That game really boosted the popularity of the Patriots."

Gino Cappelletti practices his kick in 1964. Photo courtesy of AP Images.

Nick Buoniconti, LB, 1962–1968

Most fans probably associate Buoniconti with the Miami Dolphins—he was a big name on the "No Name Defense" that won back-to-back Super Bowls and recorded the only perfect season (17–0) in modern NFL history in 1972.

Buoniconti played the first seven seasons of his 14-year professional career for the Patriots. In five of those years in Boston from 1963 to 1967, he was selected for the AFL All-Star Game and was the top vote-getter in 1966. What makes that even more impressive is that, although he had been captain of the team at Notre Dame in 1961, he wasn't drafted by the Patriots until the 13th round and wasn't drafted at all by the NFL.

Standing only 5'11" and weighing 220 pounds, he was considered too small for pro ball. That turned out to be a big mistake for all those teams that passed him up.

"His two great qualities," Dolphins coach Don Shula said, "are quickness and intelligence. He's really not tall enough to play middle linebacker, but his anticipation is so good that he's always in the right place. And he's quick as a cat."

Nick Buoniconti, pictured here in 1963, was chosen to play in the AFL All-Star Game five of his seven years with the Patriots. Photo courtesy of AP Images.

His quickness—and intelligence—served him well in the aggressive, blitzing defense preferred by Patriots coach Mike Holovak. He was highly effective both rushing the passer and dropping in pass coverage, as his 24 interceptions as a Patriot clearly show. Not bad for a guy whose "signing bonus" was a pair of season tickets for his parents who lived in Springfield, about two hours west of Boston.

Clive Rush, in yet another in a long list of examples of his cluelessness as a coach, either didn't recognize or didn't appreciate Buoniconti's considerable talents. In what ranks as the worst trade in team history, Rush dealt Buoniconti to the Dolphins for linebacker John Bramlett and quarterback Kim Hammond—both of whom were gone two years later—and a fifth-round draft choice.

Bob Dee, DE, 1960–1967

An original Patriot, this Holy Cross grad started every game—112 in a row—in his eight seasons in the AFL. He scored the first touchdown in league history when he recovered a fumble in the end zone against Buffalo in a preseason game the night of July 30, 1960. A four-time AFL All-Star, Dee had a career-high seven sacks in 14 games in 1963, when the Patriots reached the league championship game.

Jim Lee "Earthquake" Hunt, DL, 1960–1970

His nickname alone is Hall of Fame caliber. Hunt came to Boston from Prairie View, via the St. Louis Cardinals, who had drafted him and then cut him. Arriving at B.U. Field less than an hour before the Pats were to play Oakland in November 1960, Hunt was asked by coach Lou Saban, "When will you be ready to play?"

"Tonight," Hunt replied.

He then went on to play 11 seasons for the Patriots, earning All-AFL honors four times—the first in 1961, the last in 1969. He was an outstanding pass rusher, combining power and speed. He intercepted a pass against the Oilers in 1963 and returned it 78 yards for a touchdown. Among those chasing him in vain was running back Billy Cannon, who had been a Heisman Trophy winner at LSU.

Steve "Nelly" Nelson, LB, 1974–1987

Near the end of his career, Nelson said, "When I was young and could run, I didn't know where to go. Now I know where to go, but I can't get there in time."

That was typical of Nelly, a self-deprecating guy with a great sense of humor. He'd even laugh when he was reminded that even when he was young, he really couldn't run; he was hard-pressed to break five seconds in the 40.

But the fact was that he always knew where the football was to be found and usually got there before anybody else. A three-time Pro Bowl selection, he had a career-high 207 tackles in 1984, an unofficial team record. He was New England's leading tackler in eight of his 14 seasons with the club.

"He's the complete linebacker," Miami Dolphins coach Don Shula said. "He's got the savvy and the intensity. He's good against the pass and the run. He's aggressive and very intelligent."

It was Pats coach Chuck Fairbanks who said, when Nelson was a young player, that he "set a tone of toughness for the team."

That remained true throughout Nelly's career. He retired as one of the most respected and beloved players in Patriots history.

Vito "Babe" Parilli, QB, 1961–1967

Babe came to the Patriots from the Raiders in a trade after the 1960 season, which also brought capable fullback Billy Lott to Boston in exchange for halfback Dick Christy and tackle Hal Smith. It was one of the better deals in team history.

Parilli already was a well-traveled veteran by then. A collegiate star at Kentucky, where he played for the legendary Paul "Bear" Bryant, he was a first-round draft choice of the Green Bay Packers in 1952. But he struggled in Green Bay, throwing 19 interceptions and only four touchdown passes in 1953. He then was drafted by the army and spent two years in the service. When he got out he played a year in Cleveland with the Browns and then returned to Green Bay for two more seasons, backing up Bart Starr. Parilli moved to the Canadian Football League in 1959, with the Ottawa Rough Riders, then returned to the States to play in the AFL. With Oakland, he played behind a promising young quar-

Vito "Babe" Parilli, posing here in 1961, led the Patriots to the AFL Championship Game in San Diego in 1963 and held the record for passing touchdowns in a year (31) for 43 years.

terback by the name of Tom Flores, who later would coach the Raiders to a pair of Super Bowl triumphs—over the Eagles following the 1980 season and against the Redskins after the 1983 season.

Parilli had never been a full-time starter as a pro. But after sharing the job in Boston with Butch Songin for a while, he took over late in the 1961 season and remained the Patriots' No. 1 quarterback from 1962 through 1967.

He led the Pats to the AFL Championship Game in San Diego in 1963, then had his best season the following year when he threw for 31 touchdowns and 3,465 yards—both career-highs—as Boston went 10–3–1. Those 31 passing touchdowns were a franchise record until Tom Brady set an NFL record by throwing for 50 in 2007. Three times Parilli was voted to the AFL All-Star team.

Coach Mike Holovak had so much confidence in his experienced signal-caller that he let him call his own plays.

"Parilli knows exactly what he wants to do," Holovak said. "By sending in plays, all I would do is destroy the continuity of his thinking. He knows more of what's going on from the field than I do from the bench."

Traded to the Jets in 1968 for their backup quarterback, Mike Taliaferro, Parilli served as "caddy" for Joe Namath for two years and was also the holder on place kicks as he had been in Boston. He picked up a Super Bowl ring when, as Namath "guaranteed," the Jets upset the Baltimore Colts in Super Bowl III.

Mike Haynes, CB, 1976–1982

If one were to construct the perfect cornerback, he'd look like Mike Haynes—tall, sinewy-strong, fast, smart, with great hands. And throw in handsome, thoughtful, and articulate, too. It's no wonder he was elected to the Pro Football Hall of Fame in 1997.

What's unfortunate, from a New England standpoint, is that Haynes didn't finish his career with the Patriots. A contract squabble—money, or lack of it, often was the root of most evil with the Pats—led to his being traded to Oakland in midseason 1983. Haynes had been holding out, refusing to play in New England unless he received a substantially more lucrative deal than he'd been offered. At the trading deadline in October, the Patriots sent Haynes and a seventh-round pick in 1985 to Oakland for the Raiders' first-round pick in 1984 and a second-rounder in 1985.

The deal paid immediate dividends for the Raiders. With Haynes joining Lester Hayes at cornerback in Oakland, the two of them combined to shut down the Redskins' prolific receivers, Charlie Brown and Art Monk, holding that explosive duo to a total of four insignificant receptions as the Raiders romped 38–9 in Super Bowl XVIII.

"We weren't able to get our wide receivers into the offense," bemoaned Washington quarterback Joe Theismann.

It's not as if the Raiders were doing anything deceptive on defense.

"No matter what formation [the Redskins] came out in," Haynes said, "in the end it just came down to man-to-man coverage. Very basic stuff—'You take that guy, I'll take this one.' My kind of football." There have been very few of Haynes' kind of corners before or since.

Perhaps the best description of this gentlemanly athlete was provided by Hayes, who said, "Beneath that clean-shaven, boyish face lurks a man who would tear out your heart on Sunday and eat it raw."

Steve Grogan, QB, 1975–1990

When he came to the Patriots as a fifth-round draft choice out of Kansas, Grogan was a better runner than he was a passer.

"I had the arm," he said, "but I didn't use it."

The Pats were a running team in those days, as coach Chuck Fairbanks even had Grogan's predecessor, Jim Plunkett—a classic drop-back passer with a great arm but no speed or elusiveness—run the option on occasion.

Grogan took over for the battered Plunkett—who'd absorbed frightening amounts of punishment behind a porous offensive line in his

Quarterback Steve Grogan hands off in a 1980 game. His arrival brought a drastic turnaround to the Patriots, as he led a team that had been 3–11 the previous season to an 11–3 record.

four-plus seasons as a starter—midway through his rookie year. In 1976 he ran for 12 touchdowns—an NFL record for quarterbacks—in leading the Patriots to their first NFL playoff appearance. The Pats won the division title in 1978 when they rushed for 3,165 yards, a league record that's unlikely ever to be broken.

Ron Erhardt, who had been offensive coordinator for Fairbanks, could see that Grogan had possibilities as a passer and when he took over as head coach in 1979, opened up the offense. After throwing for 15 touchdowns in 1978, Grogan passed for a career-high 28 in 1979.

But the highlight of his career came in 1985. He'd lost his starting job by then to young Tony Eason, a first-round pick in 1983. But when Eason was injured in the sixth game in 1985, with the Patriots muddling along at 2–3, Grogan came off the bench and not only brought the Pats from behind to beat the Bills, but then sparked a six-game winning streak that only came to an end when he suffered a broken leg against the Jets.

With his quiet toughness, Grogan always was an inspirational leader by example, even as a young player.

"We really started to go somewhere when Steve came in," Hannah said, recalling that 1976 season when the Pats, 3–11 the year before, made a complete turnaround and went 11–3. "If you feel admiration and liking for a quarterback, you'll bust your butt for him. Everybody blocked their tail off for Grogan because they loved him."

While, like any quarterback, Grogan was booed when he threw interceptions, he was a fan favorite in New England by the time he retired after 16 seasons—the most of any player in Patriots history.

Andre Tippett, LB, 1982–1993

Andre Tippett was just starting his fifth season in the NFL, and he had one goal in mind. "I want to get into the Hall of Fame," he said. "That's where the great ones go, and I want to be there, too. From the time I came into football, my goal has been to be the best. I want to be considered the best in the business."

Even that early in his career, he had made a convincing case that he ranked right up there with the very best. Drafted in the second round in 1982 out of the University of Iowa, where he helped the Hawkeyes reach

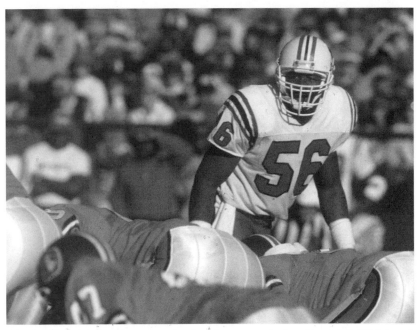

Linebacker Andre Tippett waits for the snap during the AFC Divisional Playoff Game against the Denver Broncos on January 4, 1987, at Mile High Stadium in Denver.

the Rose Bowl for the first time since 1959, Tippett led the Patriots in sacks in his second season, with 8½. But he was only warming up.

He set a franchise record with 18½ sacks in 1985, when the Pats won the AFC championship and then came back the following year and racked up 16½. He simply couldn't be blocked, not by just one man. Offensive linemen weren't fast enough to block him. Running backs weren't strong enough to block him. So what most teams did was have a tight end "chip" him at the line of scrimmage, giving a tackle time to set up and hopefully get his hands on him. The problem was that Tippett was a black belt in karate and usually could parry any attempts to latch on to his jersey. Once Tippett got past the "big guys," pity the poor running back standing between him and the quarterback. Tippett either overpowered him—practically running over him—or simply threw him aside.

The 35 sacks he had in 1985–1986 is the highest two-season total by a linebacker in NFL history. He finished his career with 100 sacks, which, needless to say, is the team record.

It was an outburst by Tippett in the locker room in Cleveland after a loss that dropped New England to 2–3 in the 1985 season that many players felt propelled the Pats to their first Super Bowl.

"He was highly emotional," running back Robert Weathers recalled. "He had tears in his eyes that day. He's usually not big on words, but he looked around the room and said, 'Look, man, I'm tired of losing. I hate losing.'

"Some of the Cleveland players," said Weathers, "were laughing at him on the way off the field. To a man like Andre Tippett, to be laughed at and not to be able to do anything about it really offends him."

The laughter unquestionably hurt and angered Tippett, but not as much as losing did. He was angry after that 24–20 setback at the hands of the Browns. He was frustrated. He was fed up. He left the field seething and, when he got into the locker room, he let his emotions come flying out with burning intensity.

"I was angry," Tippett said, "because we should have won the game. We had the opportunity to win, and we should have won. I told the guys, 'We talk about winning. We talk about going to the Super Bowl. But this isn't the way to get there. We can't let the close games get away.'

"But I said it," Tippett added with a meaningful stare, "in a more violent way. Things changed after that."

Weathers vividly remembers the change. "Coach Berry said he was with Andre all the way. It was at that point that everything turned around."

From that point on the Patriots made a dramatic turnaround, winning 12 of their next 14 games. They won three straight playoff games on the road, including a 31–14 drubbing of the defending conference champion Dolphins in the AFC Championship Game in the Orange Bowl in Miami.

"It was something that needed to be said," Tippett said of his emotional outburst in Cleveland that sparked his teammates. "Guys say after a loss, 'Don't worry, we'll get 'em next time.' I say, 'Hey, man, later for that. I've heard that bull for a long time. You don't talk like that if you really want to win.'

"If someone has to jump on people, then I say do it. If we're not playing up to our potential, I believe in letting people know. That's always been a big part of my makeup. I've always set my standards high."

The standard he set for himself, from the time he entered the NFL, was to get to the Hall of Fame. In 2008 he achieved that lifelong goal, one that had its roots on the mean streets of Newark, New Jersey, where he first began to play football and to study martial arts.

"Where I grew up," he said, "life was hard. You didn't get many things, and I had to fight for everything I got." He meant that literally.

"As a kid," Tippett said, "I used to walk past this karate school. One day I finally decided to go in. I didn't have a big brother. I didn't have anyone to rely on if I ever got into a jam. I had to learn to protect myself, so I got involved with karate.

"It was good for me physically but also mentally. It's a way of life. To succeed, you have to be able to control yourself. Karate taught me that you can do whatever you want to if you set your mind to it. It has given me a fighting spirit."

It also helped him avoid the temptations and dangers of growing up in an impoverished neighborhood. He became captain of the football, wrestling, and track teams at Barringer High and went on from there to junior college in Ellsworth, Iowa. The next step was to the University of Iowa, where, as a junior, he had 20 sacks.

He had been a stand-up defensive end for the Hawkeyes, which prompted Dick Steinberg, the Patriots' director of player development, to believe Tippett could be a highly effective pass rusher as an outside linebacker in New England's 3-4 defensive alignment.

"Andre is strong enough," Steinberg said when he drafted Tippett in the second round, "to throw blockers aside if they get in his way. He's also quick enough to avoid them, which is probably the most important thing."

Winning was the most important thing to Tippett.

"It comes down to the point where you have to produce," he said, "where you have to show what sort of man you are. I wanted to be a dominating factor. I didn't want to lose. I didn't want to be knocked down. I wanted to make the big plays. I wanted my team to be counting on me."

The Patriots always could count on Tippett in his playing days, and they still do. He serves the team now as executive director of community affairs.

Bruce Armstrong, OT, 1987–2000

The Patriots' all-time leader in games played, with 212, Armstrong appeared in six Pro Bowls and is one of only three players to have played in three decades with the same NFL team.

An exceptionally athletic tackle—he had played some tight end in college at Louisville—Armstrong excelled as a pass blocker. He took particular pride in keeping rushers away from young quarterback Drew Bledsoe's blind side.

Midway through the 1999 season, Armstrong tore ligaments in his right knee. Because the Patriots were 6–2 and battling for a playoff spot, he remained in the lineup, playing through the pain. Even when the Pats slumped in the second half of the season and were eliminated from playoff contention with two games to go, Armstrong refused to go to the sideline, wanting to do his best to ensure that Bledsoe remained healthy.

"He wanted to look out for me," Bledsoe said appreciatively. "To have a guy over there at left tackle that you can trust so completely is the ultimate luxury.

"I respect him in much the same way I respect my own father. I know if I'm in a situation where I could play but didn't, I'd have trouble looking him in the eye. There's a sense of accountability because of the way he approaches things."

Stanley "the Steamer" Morgan, WR, 1977–1989

When the newly formed Hall of Fame committee convened in the late spring of 2007, there was a speedy consensus regarding the best player not yet enshrined—the fleet wide receiver who was one of the most feared deep threats in the league throughout his career in New England.

*Stanley Morgan skillfully evades a tackle by Dallas Cowboys
linebacker Guy Brown in the fourth quarter of this game in Irving,
Texas, on December 3, 1978.* Photo courtesy of AP Images.

The Steamer was more like a rocket. He had sub-4.4 speed in the 40
and, just when it appeared that he was running full tilt, he was able to
shift into even higher gear. In each of his first five seasons with the
Patriots, after they took him in the first round out of Tennessee, the
explosive Morgan averaged more than 21 yards per catch.

Although Randy Moss set an NFL record with 23 touchdown
catches in 2007, Grogan gives Morgan the edge when pressed to say who
was the better receiver.

"They're both great," Grogan said. "They had different styles.
Randy is a big guy [6'4" and 215 pounds] with tremendous speed.
Stanley wasn't all that big [5'11" and 180 pounds], but he had speed like
nobody else I've ever seen. The difference is that Stanley would go over
the middle better than Moss does."

Ben Coates, TE, 1991–1999

Drafted out of little Livingstone (North Carolina) College in the fifth round, the 6'5", 245-pound Coates put up big numbers in New England. He led the team in receiving in five of six seasons from 1993 to 1998. Statistically his best year was 1994, when he caught 96 passes for 1,174 yards—both career highs—and seven touchdowns. At the time, those 96 receptions were an NFL record for a tight end. He scored at least six touchdowns every season for six straight years from 1993 through 1998, with a career-high of nine in 1996. He was selected for five Pro Bowls.

Quarterback Drew Bledsoe used to refer to Coates as his "security blanket." Need a completion for a first down to keep a drive alive? Throw it to Coates. Blitzers coming? Dump the ball to Coates. Trying to find the end zone? Look for Coates.

"I've always been there for Drew," Coates said. "When he's in trouble, Drew looks for me."

"What Drew shares with Ben," Pats offensive coordinator Larry Kennan said in 1997, "is a special kind of chemistry."

It helped, of course, that Coates was a special player.

"The best tight end in football," Kennan said.

Linebackers couldn't cover Coates because they weren't fast enough to run with him. Defensive backs could stay with him, but he was so much bigger that he'd either screen them from the ball or use his bulk to lean into them and bounce away, creating situations as the ball arrived from Bledsoe.

A man of few words, he never said much about his style. "If you can play," he said, "you can play."

Coates could play, no question.

chapter 9

The Big Tuna Era

Bill Parcells was hired to turn the Patriots around. And he did, taking over a team that had been 1–15 in 1990 and 2–14 in 1992, and taking them to the playoffs in 1994, then to the Super Bowl in 1996. After that he turned around and left for the Jets, leaving a bad taste and bitterness behind in New England and triggering what came to be known as the "Border War."

Parcells became the Patriots' fourth coach in five years in 1993, when he replaced Dick MacPherson, who'd missed the second half of his second season following surgery on his colon.

The personable MacPherson, who had been very successful and very popular as a college coach at Syracuse, had replaced Rod Rust following the disastrous 1990 season in which the Patriots were embarrassed both on the field and off it.

Rust had taken over from Raymond Berry. After a Super Bowl appearance in 1985 and a division title in 1986, the Pats had missed the playoffs the next two seasons, despite winning records, then fell to 5–11 in 1989. Berry resisted management demands that he make changes in his staff and was subsequently fired.

After failing to sell out a single home game and averaging less than 19 points a game, the front office insisted that Berry hire an offensive coordinator. Not an unreasonable request, considering that the Patriots scored a first-quarter touchdown in only one of their final 13 games in 1989.

"The team has not been improving for three years," general manager Patrick Sullivan said. "It has, in fact, been getting worse. We've got to make major changes to get out of this spiral."

Patriots head coach Bill Parcells discusses strategy with quarterback Drew Bledsoe during the 1994 AFC Wild Card Playoff Game against the Cleveland Browns at Cleveland Municipal Stadium.

It didn't help the situation that Dick Steinberg, the personnel expert whose shrewd drafting had brought in the talent that made the team a championship contender in the mid-1980s, had become fed up with the situation in New England and signed a lucrative contract with the Jets as director of football operations.

Berry's contract said he had the power to hire his own assistants, and he was loyal to them. So when he wouldn't make changes, management did.

"I was hired to coach the team and make coaching decisions," Berry said. "Pat's job as general manager is to make the general manager's decisions. One of those is that if he doesn't agree with the coach's decisions he can fire him. He did that. He did his job. I was doing mine."

So Rust got the job, which turned out to be a terrible decision.

"Looking back on it," Sullivan said, "I never should have fired Raymond. It probably was the biggest mistake I ever made."

A case could be made that hiring Rust was a bigger mistake. Well respected as a defensive coordinator, Rust wasn't cut out to be a head coach in the NFL.

The Patriots lost their opener in 1990 by a field goal to Miami, then beat the Colts in Indianapolis. But that was followed by a 41–7 drubbing at Cincinnati—the first of what would turn out to be a franchise-record 14 consecutive losses. In 10 of them the Patriots failed to score more than 10 points. The 24 points they scored in the first game of the year against the Dolphins turned out to be their season high.

Lack of talent was the team's major problem. But there also was another issue: lack of character.

Among the writers on the Patriots beat that season was a young woman working for the *Boston Herald*, Lisa Olson. She was interviewing cornerback Maurice Hurst in the locker room the day after New England's win at Indianapolis when several naked players gathered around her and began making obscene comments and gestures. The incident led to an investigation by the league in which players were asked which of their teammates were involved. It was a highly disruptive and hugely embarrassing situation for a team that already was embarrassing itself on the field.

An upshot of the incident, which received national publicity, was that team owner Victor Kiam hired University of Miami athletic director Sam Jankovich to take control of the Patriots' football operation. Jankovich quickly moved to fire Rust and hire MacPherson.

"I wanted an upbeat, aggressive, enthusiastic guy," Jankovich said. He got that. What he didn't get was a guy who could make the Patriots winners. Surprisingly the Pats won six games in 1991, Coach Mac's first season on the job. But they lost their first nine games in 1992, at which point MacPherson became ill and wasn't able to return until the final game of the season, which the Pats lost in overtime to Miami, finishing the year 2–14.

Beset by financial woes, Kiam had sold the team to James Busch Orthwein in the spring of 1992. It was widely assumed at the time that Orthwein, a native of St. Louis who was related on his mother's side to the Busch brewing family had bought the Patriots with the idea of moving them to his hometown, which had lost the Cardinals to Arizona in 1988.

Orthwein stated that he would "not be the Patriots owner indefi- nitely," but as long as he was in control he "would be involved actively in improving the franchise."

He did that in dramatic fashion by hiring Parcells, who had stepped down as coach of the New York Giants after winning his second Super Bowl in 1990.

"I don't envision making the Patriots a competitive team," Parcells said. "I envision making the Patriots a championship team. I'm not interested in improving this team a little bit to the point where it can be competitive from week to week. I'm interested in improving this team to the point where it can contend for the championship of the National Football League. That's the only goal a guy like me can have in this coaching profession."

It was a goal Parcells achieved quickly. It helped that he inherited the first pick in the 1993 draft and, needing a quarterback, used it to select Drew Bledsoe of Washington State rather than Rick Mirer of Notre Dame. Mirer also was well regarded but turned out to be nowhere near as good.

Bledsoe immediately was installed as the starter, and although the Patriots lost 11 of their first 12 games under Parcells, they won their last four games of the 1993 season, creating optimism for the upcoming year.

That optimism proved to be justified as the Pats overcame a 3–6 start by winning their last seven games and earning a wild-card spot in the playoffs. Playing in Cleveland on New Year's Day, they lost 20–13 to Bill Belichick's Browns.

The 1995 season was disappointing, as the Patriots slipped to 6–10. But after losing the first two games in 1996, the Pats put everything together and rolled to their first division title in 10 years, posting a record of 11–5. That earned them their first home playoff game since 1978, when, in disarray over the impending departure of Chuck Fairbanks, the Patriots were routed by the Oilers. Little did the 1996 Patriots know their coach was on the way out, too.

The conference semifinal against Pittsburgh was played in a thick fog in which the Steelers appeared lost.

Pittsburgh received the opening kickoff, but went three-and-out. On came the Steelers' defense, an aggressive group that people were calling "Blitzburgh" because of the frequency and intensity with which they rushed the passer.

But it was Bledsoe who went right after the Steelers, lofting a 53-yard bomb to Terry Glenn on the first play and sending Curtis Martin into the end zone from the 2 on the next.

"That changed the whole game, right there," wide receiver Shawn Jefferson said. "That first play swung the momentum. That put us on a roll."

The Patriots proceeded to steamroll the Steelers, opening a 21–0 lead less than 20 minutes into the game. Running back Keith Byars took a 34-yard screen pass from Bledsoe all the way to the end zone on the Patriots' second possession, and the Pats scored again on a game-breaking—and, for the Steelers, morale-breaking—78-yard touchdown run by Martin. Pittsburgh never did get into the New England end zone, and the final score was 28–3.

The Patriots had been expecting, had they won, a trip to Denver for the AFC Championship Game. They weren't looking forward to it. The Pats hadn't won in the Mile High City since 1968, losing nine in a row. Actually, it really didn't seem to matter where the Patriots played the Broncos. They'd been blown out by them in Foxboro two months earlier, 34–8, and had lost 11 straight to Denver. John Elway, the Broncos' future Hall of Fame quarterback, had a lifetime 9–0 record against the Pats. So great joy and great relief abounded in New England when the Broncos were upset 30–27 by Jacksonville.

The Jaguars consequently came to Foxboro and came close to upsetting the Patriots, too. Instead of a blowout from the outset, as the Pittsburgh game had been, the AFC Championship Game was in doubt deep into the fourth quarter. It wasn't until—with the Patriots clinging tenaciously and tenuously to a 13–6 lead—the appropriately nicknamed Willie "Big Play" Clay intercepted a pass in the end zone that the Pats were able to lock up their second trip to the Super Bowl.

New England never trailed, seizing a 7–0 lead in the first quarter on a one-yard touchdown run by Martin. But after that the teams traded field goals, Adam Vinatieri booting two for New England and Mike Hollis kicking a pair for Jacksonville.

The Jags appeared to be on the brink of tying the score when, with 3:43 left to play, they had a second-and-goal at the 5. Quarterback Mark Brunell thought he saw tight end Derek Brown open in the end zone. He never saw Clay.

"I didn't see the back-side safety," Brunell said. "He stepped right in front of the pass. The interception in the end zone—that was it, right there. That was the turnover that really hurt us."

Jacksonville did get the ball back once more and turned it over again. New England defensive back Otis Smith picked up a fumble and ran 47 yards for a touchdown to make the final score 20–6, but it was Big Play Clay who saved the day.

There was a two-week break before the Super Bowl, but the upcoming game wasn't the primary topic of conservation in New England. Instead, the focus was on the feeling that Parcells was about to leave to take over the Jets because of a deterioration of relations with team owner Robert Kraft.

The simple reason for the lack of amity between coach and owner was that Parcells didn't have the complete control over personnel he insisted he needed to make the Patriots consistent winners. Parcells complained that Kraft wanted him "to cook the dinner" but wouldn't allow him "to shop for the groceries." But the problems between the two went deeper than that.

"I was fortunate," Kraft said, "to come in and have one of the great coaches in the game. But he really wasn't my kind of guy. I want people who think long-term. Bill is a great coach, but he wasn't willing to make a long-term commitment to the organization.

"With the salary cap, I've got to make personnel decisions thinking two and three years ahead. He was only interested in coaching year-to-year. At the end of every year, he'd drive to Florida, saying he'd let me know when he got there if he'd be coming back."

It wasn't as if Kraft and Parcells spent a lot of time chatting, even when the coach was in his office in Foxboro. "He wasn't always respectful about telling me what was going on," Kraft said.

So there was all sorts of "extracurricular" stuff going on the week of Super Bowl XXXI in New Orleans. Coaches hate distractions, especially before a big game. But the Big Tuna had become one whale of a distraction as the Patriots prepared to play the Packers. The players insisted they were focused.

"It's not affecting us at all," linebacker Willie McGinest said. "Our job is to play football. His job is to prepare us to play. He's not a distraction. The distractions are out on Bourbon Street."

"I haven't thought about it twice," said linebacker Chris Slade, who was asked about it more often than that in the week leading up to the game. "We've been hearing that [Parcells might leave] throughout the course of the season—'Is he going? Is he staying?'

"I look at it like him being a player. It's like he's a free agent now after four years here. He can go to another team, or he can stay."

But for former New England linebacker Steve Nelson, the situation was eerily similar to 1978, when it came out prior to the playoffs that coach Chuck Fairbanks would be bailing on the team to go to the University of Colorado.

When Fairbanks left, Nelson said, "It divided the team. There were players who loved Fairbanks, and there were those who were glad to see him go."

It wasn't what the Patriots needed, going up against a Green Bay team that led the NFL in both points scored and fewest points allowed.

"I'd say it was a little bit of a distraction all the way around," Belichick told former *Boston Globe* sportswriter Michael Holley for his book *Patriot Reign*. "I can tell you firsthand, there was a lot of stuff going on prior to the game. I mean, him talking to [the Jets]. He was trying to make up his mind about what he wanted to do. Which, honestly, I felt totally inappropriate. How many chances do you get to play for the Super Bowl? Tell them to get back to you in a couple of days. I'm not saying it was disrespectful to me, but it was in terms of the overall commitment to the team."

As it turned out, the Patriots played very respectably. The difference in the game was a 99-yard kickoff return by Green Bay's Desmond Howard in the third quarter. This came after the Patriots, who'd fallen behind 10–0 early and trailed 27–14 at halftime, cut their deficit to 27–21 on an 18-yard run by Martin.

Any momentum they may have had was quickly erased when Howard took the ensuing kickoff all the way to the end zone. That made the score 34–21, and that was the way the game ended.

But the drama surrounding Parcells was only just beginning. He didn't fly home with the team after the game—something else that bothered Belichick. Then he went flying off to the Jets, causing Kraft to demand compensation in the way of draft picks in return for his coach.

He got 'em—a third and a fourth in 1997, a second-round choice in 1998, and a first-round pick in 1999. Considering what the Patriots wound up getting with those picks, it appears Parcells was right to complain that he should have been allowed to "shop for the groceries."

In 1997 the Pats chose running back Sedrick Shaw and offensive lineman Damon Denson with picks they'd gotten for Parcells. In 1998 they selected wide receiver Tony Simmons. They used their first-round choice from New York in 1999 to take linebacker Andy Katzenmoyer. None of those four players wound up making any significant contribution to the team.

Needless to say, there was acrimony and animosity aplenty when the Jets came to Foxboro the following fall on the second Sunday in September for the first of what would become known as the Tuna Bowls.

The Patriots won 27–24 in overtime, but the Jets won four of the next five, which contributed to the demise of Parcells' successor in New England, Pete Carroll, who ironically had been coach of the Jets for one year (1994) before being fired.

Although Carroll never had a losing season with the Patriots, the team's record got worse every year, slipping to 10–6 in 1997, when they lost in the conference semifinals; to 9–7 in 1998, when they lost in the opening round of the playoffs; and to 8–8 in 1999, when they failed to make the playoffs. That's when he was fired and Belichick was hired.

This time it was the Jets who received compensation from Kraft and the Patriots for hiring away the man they thought was going to be their head coach.

It was Parcells, who'd moved to the front office in New York, who broke the three-year silence with Kraft that had lent the aura of a Hatfields-and-McCoys-type feud to the so-called Border Wars.

"I told [Kraft] it was Darth Vader calling," Parcells said. "He said he knew who that was. We had a chance to talk amiably. We had a few laughs about things that had happened in the past, some things I think we're both sorry happened. There are a few things I did that I wish I could do over again. That's life. He was a new owner. I was an older coach. Sometimes that's hard."

Pat Patriot

It was a sad day in franchise history when Pat Patriot was let go.

After 32 years of adorning the helmets of the Boston, then briefly Bay State, and finally New England Patriots, Pat was unceremoniously dumped after the 1992 season.

In place of the quirky Colonial crouching over the ball, ready to snap it, the Patriots adopted a slick, modernized version of a Patriot who looked like a cross between Elvis in a tricorn hat and the FTD delivery logo.

"We know," said James Orthwein, who purchased the franchise from Victor Kiam in the spring of 1992, "that there will be those who will protest this change. One does not lightly approach changing a team icon. We know we are dealing with a proud history, with memories that are important to us all. But memories are like looking in the rearview mirror as you drive forward. You can't focus on what's behind. You have to anticipate what lies ahead. We look at this change as evolutionary, not revolutionary."

Pat Patriot may have been a cartoon character—he was the creation of *Boston Globe* artist Phil Bissell—but his presence on the helmets of the Patriots was a serious matter to New England's football fans, who took him to their hearts.

Pat's popularity was evidenced early in the 1979 season, when team founder Billy Sullivan's marketing mavens decided it was time for a new mascot.

Being a native of Massachusetts, the cradle of democracy, where voting early and voting often have been time-honored traditions from the earliest days of the Commonwealth, Sullivan felt it only right to put the not-insignificant matter of changing mascots up to the paying customers. So a vote was held on a sunny Sunday afternoon in September at Schaefer Stadium.

Pat, looking very much like one of those battle-worn figures in the famous *Spirit of '76* painting, was up against a spit-and-polish NFL Properties–designed figure dubbed "Super Patriot."

The league, if not exactly the Family Sullivan, were hoping—indeed, expecting—Super Patriot to win handily, thus creating new marketing opportunities. They were disappointed when Pat won in a landslide. His place in the hearts of Patriots fans made obvious, he retained his position on the team's helmets for almost another quarter-century.

But with the Patriots coming off a 2–14 season, two years after they'd been 1–15, and with sales of team merchandise ranking a lowly 26th (of 28 teams), Orthwein cast the only vote that mattered—Pat was out.

Nor was that the only change. In place of their traditional red-colored home jerseys and white pants, the Patriots were switching to blue jerseys with silver pants.

"We're not making these changes as a substitute for improving our team," Orthwein said. "We're doing it in conjunction with improving our team. I believe we improved our product immensely when we hired Bill Parcells. This is an improvement in the packaging of that product."

Parcells, who knew much more about football than fashion, grumblingly went along with the changes.

"I don't really care about uniforms that make players look good," he said. "I want players who make uniforms look good."

As it turned out, Pat made a brief—and successful—comeback.

On what the NFL called a "Throwback Weekend" in September 1994, where teams reverted to older uniforms, Pat sparked the Patriots, who had lost their first two games, to a 31–28 victory at Cincinnati. Two weeks later he was in action again—this time in front of the home fans in Foxboro Stadium. Undoubtedly inspired by his presence and the enthusiastic cheers of the home crowd, the Patriots won again, defeating the Packers 17–16.

Pat made his final appearance of the season two weeks after that against the Jets in a 24–17 loss at the Meadowlands. Then he was done, sent back into retirement. Although given his 2–1 record, compared to the 1–3 mark compiled by Elvis to that point, there were more than a few New England fans who thought Pat should have been allowed to stick around.

Bledsoe

For Drew Bledsoe the 2001 AFC Championship Game in Pittsburgh was a day of jubilation and vindication. That was the season he went from being a franchise quarterback to a backup quarterback.

Once he had been the cornerstone of the Patriots' future. By the end of 2001 he was on the brink of becoming just another part of the past. He had been the first player taken in the 1993 draft and immediately became not only the starting quarterback in New England, taking over a team that had gone 2–14 the year before, but also the face of the franchise.

That was Bill Parcells' first year as coach of the Patriots, and he decided early on that if the team could be turned around, the strong-armed young quarterback out of Washington State was the man to do it. He was, and he did.

The turning point came midway through the 1994 season with the Patriots—who'd been 5–11 in Bledsoe's rookie year after losing 11 of their first 12—muddling along at 3–6 and trailing the Minnesota Vikings 20–0 late in the first half in Foxboro.

The Pats had lost four in a row, hadn't scored a touchdown in their previous two games, and, after making a first down on their first play against the Vikes, didn't make another until the final minute of the first half. That was when the Pats went to a hurry-up offense and Bledsoe started to throw. And throw. And throw.

He threw 70 times in all, including 34 times in a row in the second half and overtime. He threw on the last two plays of the third quarter and on every play—all 27 of them—in the fourth quarter, at the end of which the Patriots had tied the game at 20–20. The Patriots won the toss in overtime, and Bledsoe threw five more times before the Pats finally ran a running play.

Fittingly the final play of the game was a pass; Bledsoe, who was 7-for-7 in the game-winning 68-yard drive, threw 14 yards to running back Kevin Turner for a touchdown.

He finished with an NFL-record 45 completions in an NFL-record 70 attempts for 426 yards and three touchdowns. What he didn't throw, amazingly, was an interception. Nor was he sacked, as the Patriots ran their two-minute offense for the final two quarters.

Quarterback Drew Bledsoe drops back behind his offensive line after taking the snap during the first quarter of the Patriots' 17–3 victory over the Miami Dolphins in the AFC Wild Card Playoff Game at Foxboro Stadium on December 28, 1997. Photo courtesy of AP Images.

Bledsoe threw. Somebody would catch. The Pats would run up to the point of completion. They'd line up, snap the ball, and he'd throw it again. Throw it. Catch it. Run up. Line up. Snap it. Throw it. "Drew likes that kind of thing," Parcells said.

"I've always enjoyed the two-minute offense," Bledsoe concurred. "In football camp, every summer when I was a kid, we'd always have a two-minute drill at the end of the day. We'd get the high tempo going. You didn't have to stand around and wait between throws. You're in control of what you're throwing."

After that exciting comeback, that marvelous passing exhibition, the Patriots didn't lose again the rest of the regular season, going on a seven-game winning streak that left them 10–6 and in possession of the franchise's first playoff berth in eight years.

Although they lost 20–13 to Bill Belichick's Browns in Cleveland in the opening round, the Patriots, with Bledsoe at quarterback, clearly were headed in the right direction.

Two years later they were in the Super Bowl, where they trailed Brett Favre and the Green Bay Packers by only a touchdown in the third quarter before Desmond Howard broke the game open with a 99-yard kickoff return for the decisive and final touchdown in a 35–21 Green Bay victory.

Parcells left then, Pete Carroll came in, but Bledsoe continued to lead the team, taking the Patriots to a second straight division title in 1997 and a third straight playoff berth in 1998—their fourth in five years.

But the Pats had gone from 11–5 in Parcells' final season to 10–6 in Carroll's first, then 9–7 in 1998. When the slide continued to 8–8 and no playoffs in 1999, Carroll was gone.

Belichick took over and stuck with Bledsoe through a disappointing 5–11 season in 2000. That was the year the Patriots drafted a skinny quarterback out of Michigan by the name of Tom Brady in Round 6.

When Bledsoe was injured in the second game of the 2001 season, dealt a devastating blow that sheared a blood vessel in his chest by Jets linebacker Mo Lewis, Brady took over and Bledsoe never got back into the lineup.

Until the AFC Championship Game in Pittsburgh, that is. He didn't think he was going to play in that game either. Which is why, when he took the final snap from center Damien Woody, he remained down on one knee, a myriad of thoughts running through his mind. His teammates began jumping up and down, celebrating the victory he had come off the bench to lead them to—a decisive, upset win that put the Pats in the Super Bowl.

While his ears filled with the sounds of jubilation and his eyes filled with tears, one image after another from the most difficult, frustrating season of his career flashed through his mind. He thought of Dick Rehbein, the Patriots' quarterbacks coach who died suddenly of heart disease at the start of training camp. He thought of how the Patriots had lost their first two games—the only two games he'd played that season. He thought of the hit by Lewis that sidelined him for two months. He thought of how, when he finally was ready to return, Belichick told him that the job he'd held since his first game as a rookie no longer belonged to him. He thought about his father, Mac, who had been his coach in high school and who had agonized over his son's demotion. And he thought of how, as unlikely a prospect as it had seemed, he had prepared himself to play.

"I'd been working hard and preparing for that exact scenario," he said. "That's the way you have to prepare. I knew, if it came up, I was going to be able to come in and play well.

"To have that happen—to be kneeling with the ball at the end of the game, knowing we were going to the Super Bowl—was overwhelming."

The Patriots were nursing a 7–3 lead, courtesy of a 55-yard punt return for a touchdown by Troy Brown, with just under two minutes remaining in the first half, when Brady twisted his knee when he was hit by a blitzing defensive back just after completing a 28-yard pass to Brown at the Steelers' 40-yard line.

As Brady limped to the sideline, Bledsoe strapped on his helmet and, for the first time since the second week of the season, ran on to the field. "I was pretty fired up when I got out there," he said.

He could have been forgiven for misfiring on his first few passes, not only because he hadn't played in months, but also because the Pittsburgh defense had given up fewer yards than any team in the NFL and fewer points than any team in the AFC.

Instead he fired a 15-yard completion to wide receiver David Patten on his first play. On the next play, unable to find an open man, Bledsoe scrambled out of the pocket and toward the right sideline, where, in a play eerily reminiscent of the one on which he'd been injured, he was hit by defensive back Chad Scott.

"That might have been a positive thing," said Bledsoe, who bounced right up and ran quickly back to the huddle. "To take a hit when you haven't played in a while, sometimes it kinds of helps you get going."

Having run for four yards, Bledsoe kept the drive going by throwing to Patten again for 11 yards, to the 10. Then he went back to him again, lofting a perfect pass to the right rear corner of the end zone for a touchdown and a 14–3 halftime lead.

"Drew did a great job," Patten said. "All he wanted was the opportunity to help the team win. When it came, he was ready and took advantage of it."

"You've got to give him a lot of credit," said Charlie Weis, who was the Patriots' offensive coordinator. "He earned a pat on the back."

He got one from Belichick. "I can't say enough," said Belichick, "about the job Drew did. He stepped in there cold when Tom rolled his ankle and made a couple of big throws. Then he hit a couple more in the fourth quarter to keep drives moving. You have to give him a lot of credit. That was a terrific performance under pressure."

It turned out to be Bledsoe's last performance in a Patriots uniform. The following spring he was traded to Buffalo—a bit of a slap in the face because Belichick obviously wasn't worried by the prospect of having to face his former quarterback twice a year in the AFC East.

"It was a long year for me personally," Bledsoe said of that 2001 season, "starting back in training camp with the loss of my quarterback coach. Then to start out 0–2 and get injured and not be able to get back on the field—all those things made for a very long year.

"The hardest part for me was not playing. With my makeup, all of the other outside stuff that goes with being an NFL quarterback never really appealed to me. What I enjoyed was playing the game. It was hard, not being able to go on the field and play the game I love."

Instead of being disruptive, complaining about how he was being ill-treated, sniping at Brady, he was supportive. His teammates recognized that and greatly appreciated it.

"To be a franchise quarterback and then, all of a sudden, nothing— I don't know if I could have handled myself the way he did," veteran linebacker Tedy Bruschi said. "It was a testament to his character.

"He was the player who showed me how to be unselfish and really put the team first. No one really remembers what Drew Bledsoe went through that year. How would that affect you when you had a job, and you did it very well, and all of a sudden it's taken away from you? How would you react?

"The way Drew reacted was, 'I'm going to help this kid out and put the team first.' I hope that's an example a lot of people remember when you think of that team—Drew Bledsoe's example of being unselfish."

chapter 9

Bill Belichick

He's on his way to becoming a coaching legend. Some might say—and, at least in New England, there aren't many who'd argue—Bill Belichick is already there. Right there with Vince Lombardi and Bill Walsh; with Chuck Noll and Don Shula; with Paul Brown and Tom Landry; with George "Papa Bear" Halas and his old boss with the Giants, Jets, and Patriots—Bill Parcells.

In nine seasons as head coach of the Patriots, Belichick has been to four Super Bowls and won three of them. He's won six division titles, including five in a row from 2003 through 2007, and taken the team to five AFC Championship Games. He's twice had winning streaks of 21 consecutive games—one, including postseason games, in 2003–04; the other, counting only regular-season games, extending from 2006 into 2008.

He hasn't had a losing season in New England since his first, in 2000, when the Patriots were 5–11. Since then they've finished over .500 eight years in a row. While winning back-to-back NFL championships in 2003–04, the Patriots were 34–4 overall. In 2006–07, they were 32–6.

In 2007 the Patriots became only the second team in modern NFL history to finish the regular season undefeated, 16–0, and came within seconds of completing a perfect season before the Giants, Belichick's old team, snatched it away.

If, as Parcells likes to say, you are what your record says you are, then Belichick clearly is the best coach in the game today and arguably one of the best in NFL history.

Is there anyone who could have predicted that? Not anyone who saw his rambling, Captain Queeg–like press conference the day he submitted his resignation on a small, crumpled piece of paper as "HC of the NYJ." Not anyone who saw how things crumbled around him in Cleveland, where he was reviled rather than revered. And certainly not anyone who saw him as a 24-year-old tight-ends coach with the Detroit Lions in 1976, the year after he'd graduated from Wesleyan College.

"The reason he got that job," recalled Jon Morris, a seven-time AFL All-Star at center for the Patriots from 1964 to 1970, "was that Rick Forzano, who was the coach in Detroit, had been head coach at Navy, where Bill's father, Steve, was an assistant for many years.

"When I went to Detroit back in the days when they actually used to win a few games now and then, it was a veteran team. They'd been playing together for a long time. Most of the guys couldn't stand Forzano.

"He brought in Bill, who in those days was captain of the 'all-awkward' squad. He couldn't relate to anybody, for any reason.

"Most of the players were older than he was. He'd never played pro ball. He had no social graces. Guys would tease him in the locker room about being 'the coach's son.'

"During training camp that summer," said Morris, "he was pretty much a gofer. He'd go back and forth to the airport, dropping guys off or picking them up. He also was 'the Turk'—the guy who'd have to tell a player he'd been cut and get the playbook back from him.

"When the season started, they had to have something else for him to do, so they made him tight-ends coach. We only had two tight ends, and one of them—Charlie Sanders—was a Hall of Famer.

"On the practice field, Bill would tell his guys to block down on the linebacker or whatever it is coaches tell tight ends to do. But every time he said something, guys would mock him.

"That wasn't right. I felt badly for him. He was a young guy trying to get started and was a very hard worker."

Dick Jauron, now the coach of the Buffalo Bills, was a defensive back for the Lions when Belichick arrived.

"We were both very young at the time," Jauron said, "and obviously, in different areas of the organization, so I didn't spend a lot of time with

Bill Belichick paces the sideline during the second quarter of the Patriots' AFC conference game against the Pittsburgh Steelers on September 9, 2002. Photo courtesy of AP Images.

him off the field. But you could see that he was very dedicated and clearly very bright. He was very focused on the game, trying to learn everything he could from the other staff members. He was very serious and very smart."

It was Belichick's work ethic that Morris couldn't help but notice and admire.

"I liked him," Morris said, "because he worked his butt off. His primary job with the Lions was to break film down, and he'd spend eight, 10, 12 hours a day doing that.

"A few years ago, after the Patriots had won the Super Bowl, I saw Jim Yarbrough, who was an offensive tackle on that Lions team. I asked him, 'Did you ever think Belichick would be such a successful head coach?' Yarbrough laughed and said, 'I didn't even think he'd be a successful tight-ends coach.'"

Belichick earned a reputation as a defensive genius with the Giants, who won two Super Bowls when he was Parcells' defensive coordinator.

That earned him his first head coaching job, in Cleveland, where he was hardly a rousing success. He did manage to get the Browns to the playoffs in 1994—when they beat Parcells' Patriots in the opening round in Cleveland—but he had four losing seasons in five years and his drafts and free-agent signings weren't very good, so when owner Art Modell moved the franchise to Baltimore he didn't take Belichick along with him.

To say he wasn't popular in Cleveland is putting it mildly. Very few of his players liked him. Very few people in the Browns' front office liked him. The fans hated him because he'd replaced their hometown hero, Bernie Kosar, at quarterback with Vinny Testaverde. And nobody in the media liked him.

In the book *Patriot Reign* by Michael Holley, Belichick talked about his problems with the Cleveland media.

"When I got there," he said, "there had been a very open media policy from previous regimes. They had open practice, open locker rooms, pretty much whatever they wanted, to the point where the players really had no privacy. You know, a guy would play a joke on somebody or say something, and it would be in the paper the next day. There was no real opportunity for the team to build much of its own personality or chemistry because that stuff was reported on a daily basis.

"I clamped down on them. It could have been done in a more positive or gracious way. I could have made some concessions so that it wouldn't have come off as being so harsh. I take responsibility for it. But the bottom line was we just didn't win quickly enough. The media logic was, 'Okay, you want to come in and close practices and limit our access and give us some short answers? You had better start putting up some wins.' And when that didn't happen, with three consecutive losing seasons, there wasn't a great defense mechanism built up there.

"But I was kind of oblivious to that, too. Because I really was more concerned about coaching the team than trying to be a P.R. machine."

What P.R. Belichick got wasn't good. There were jokes around town about how he was the first person to successfully survive a charisma bypass operation and that when we went into a bar during happy hour he was asked to leave because he was spoiling the mood.

"When he left Cleveland I didn't think he'd get another job as a head coach," said defensive end Anthony Pleasant, who would play for Belichick not only with the Browns but also with the Jets in New York and then in New England.

"There was so much negative publicity around what happened there, I thought it would be hard for another owner to hire him. He did some things that didn't go over very well. He didn't listen to anybody. He didn't relate to the players. It was always, 'This is the way we did it in New York, and this is the way we're doing it here.'

"He's not like that anymore. He's not a know-it-all with a chip on his shoulder like he was with the Browns. He's not the same person. He learned from his mistakes."

When he was fired in Cleveland, Parcells wasted no time hiring him as his assistant head coach with the Patriots. When Parcells went to the Jets in 1997, Belichick went with him.

When Parcells decided to step down after the 1999 season, Belichick was waiting in the wings to step in and take over. Except that, as it turned out, he didn't want the job, even though he had a signed contract to coach the team.

At a bizarre press conference on January 4, 2000, Belichick, looking even more disheveled than usual and appearing to be disoriented, launched into a rambling, voice-cracking, 25-minute explanation of why he would not be coaching the Jets.

He voiced concerns about the team's unsettled ownership situation at the time. Left unsaid was the concern that Parcells would be looking over his shoulder. It was a surreal scene, prompting Jets president Steve Gutman to question Belichick's mental stability.

"We should have some sorrow and regret for him and his family," Gutman said after Belichick left the podium. "He obviously has some inner turmoil."

There would be some very public turmoil in the weeks to come, as the Patriots proceeded to try to bring Belichick to New England to replace Pete Carroll, who'd taken over after Parcells bailed on the Pats to coach the Jets.

Parcells' abrupt departure in the wake of winning the AFC championship in 1996 was the opening salvo in what would become known as the Border Wars—a tiff that turned the Jets and Pats into the Hatfields and McCoys, feuding neighbors in two of the country's largest media markets.

The Jets paid a large ransom for Parcells, giving jilted owner Robert Kraft's club a third- and fourth-round choice in 1997, a second-round pick in 1998, and a first-rounder in 1999.

The Patriots wound up wasting all of them, selecting Sedrick Shaw and Damon Denson in 1997, Tony Simmons in 1998, and Andy Katzenmoyer in 1999. But that's another story.

What's pertinent here is that the Patriots had to give the Jets a first-round pick in 2000 after signing Belichick, which turned out to be the bargain of the century. At the time, though, it was hard to figure what Kraft saw in Belichick.

"It's my job," Kraft said, "to see things that other people don't. I thought he was one of the finest football minds I'd ever encountered. It was amazing to me that no one else had hired him. But I was roundly criticized when I did."

Kraft's decision to hire Belichick was based on much more than Xs and Os. "I have certain qualities I look for when I'm hiring someone," Kraft said. "I look first at integrity, character, and loyalty. That's most important. No. 2 is work ethic. No. 3, I look at brains. If they don't have one and two, brains don't matter. Bill had all those qualities." And more.

"Another part of it," Kraft said of his decision to hire Belichick, "is a chemistry I personally feel. When Bill was here in '96 with Parcells, we developed what I call 'simpatico.' He impressed me a great deal. I'd watched him and the way he worked, and I sensed I'd be able to support him and help him in ways that would allow him to flourish."

He certainly has flourished. But he's still as hard to read as one of his defenses.

The late David Halberstam, who, in terms of talents, was to journalists what Belichick is to football coaches, spent many hours with him on Nantucket for a book titled *The Education of a Coach*. In the end what Halberstam came away with was this description of Belichick: "What a curious, complicated, contradictory man, a hard man to reach and to understand."

What should be understood from the outset is that Belichick grew up in the game. His father, Steve, played professionally for the Detroit Lions and went on to become an assistant at Navy, where he became not only a coach but also practically an institution.

He was at the Naval Academy from 1956 through 1989. Throughout those years his primary responsibility was to scout the opposition and prepare the Midshipmen for what they could expect to see in their next game.

"Every Monday," Steve Belichick told me in the press box before the Army-Navy game in Philadelphia in 2001, "I'd give a scouting report to the players on our upcoming game. I'd show them film and diagram plays."

At many of those meetings he was accompanied by his only child, Bill, even when the boy was as young as nine years old.

"He used to spend a lot of time with me," Steve said. "I'd draw up plays on the blackboard, and he'd sit there watching and listening. He started breaking down film for me when he was 10. He would diagram the plays, too. He was a hell of a lot neater than I was. He was always meticulous about it."

So it should have been no surprise to Steve that Bill would follow his father into coaching. But it was.

"He never told me he wanted to coach," Steve said, "until the second semester of his senior year in college."

Bill was at Wesleyan then. He had gone to high school in Annapolis, Maryland, then spent a year in prep school at the prestigious Philips Andover Academy in Massachusetts, where he played football and lacrosse.

He continued to play both sports at Wesleyan, lettering as a center on the football team and as a midfielder and attackman on the lacrosse team.

"Bill was a better lacrosse player than he was a football player," said Bill Devereaux, a hockey and lacrosse player at Wesleyan, where he also was Belichick's roommate. "In football he was an average Division III player. In lacrosse he was better than that. He was the captain his senior year.

"He was a student of both sports. On both teams there was the feeling that having Bill was like having a coach on the field."

And what was it like having Belichick as a roommate?

"He was a little laid-back, but he was a regular guy," Devereaux said. "He always had the ability to get by on very little sleep. He also was unflappable. Once, when we were freshmen, me and another guy threw a couple of firecrackers into the room and he never even came out."

Devereaux isn't surprised that Belichick became a successful head coach, although he didn't think he was rooming with a guy who'd win three Super Bowls.

"The guys who played football with him aren't shocked at where Bill is today," he said. "He always had a great work ethic, and no one knew the game better than he did."

Even as a kid, his father said, Bill didn't sleep very much. "He's never needed a lot of sleep," Steve Belichick said. "We'd let him stay up late when he was a kid, but you'd never catch him in bed after 8:00."

When Bill told his dad he wanted to coach after college, Steve called Lou Holtz at North Carolina State. Holtz had been an assistant at Connecticut under Forzano. It was arranged for Bill to become a graduate assistant for the Wolfpack. That lasted until the NCAA passed a rule cutting back on the size of coaching staffs, at which point Bill began to think about the NFL. He landed a job with the Colts, who were coached by Ted Marchibroda during that fall of 1975.

"They played six preseason games in those days," Steve said. "Before the end of the summer, Bill was breaking down film and doing the scouting reports for the defensive coaches. They told me they didn't have to do a darn thing.

"He started out working for nothing. Halfway through the season they gave him $25 a week. By the end of the year he was getting $50."

He'd been offered a lot more money, coming out of Wesleyan, by Proctor & Gamble, but it was the football business that intrigued Bill Belichick. When he joined the staff of the Lions in 1976, his career path was established.

"Early on," Steve said, "he was younger than a lot of the players he was coaching. But they knew he knew what he was talking about." His father knew that if intelligence, diligence, and work ethic meant anything, his son would be a success. "He's smarter than hell," Steve said.

"He inherited his mother's intelligence. He's got a real good mind. And he's very organized."

That combination of intelligence and organization has proven tough to beat.

"He's so thorough," said longtime Patriots assistant Dante Scarnecchia, who has worked for Ron Meyer, Raymond Berry, Dick MacPherson, Bill Parcells, Pete Carroll, and now Belichick over the course of 25 seasons in New England. "He always makes it clear what he wants, and he doesn't miss anything."

"He points out things you'd never even think about," quarterback Tom Brady said.

Like a chess master, Belichick always seems to be several moves ahead of his opponent.

"He always seems to be at least two steps ahead," said Charlie Weis, who was Belichick's offensive coordinator on the Patriots' three NFL championship teams before leaving after the 2004 season to become head coach at his alma mater, Notre Dame.

"It's not just Xs and Os," Weis said. "It's personnel. It's the whole organization. I think that gives him a decisive edge over most people he's going against. There are a lot of people who are good at Xs and Os, but there are very few people who have the insight, the foresight, to look ahead and try to figure out what to do before situations even come up."

His players appreciate being well prepared. They also appreciate how much time Belichick spends in preparation to get them ready.

"Every time I see him, whether it is 5:30 or 6:00 in the morning or 10:00 at night, he's always in his office," veteran safety Rodney Harrison said. "I've never seen him sit down in the cafeteria and have a decent meal. I just see him grab some chips and poke them in his mouth and keep moving. He is a different [type of] man. To me, he is so bent on attention to detail."

Belichick says he paid too much attention to detail in Cleveland.

"I'm a detail-oriented person, and I probably had a tendency to do too much," he said "I've definitely delegated more in New England.

"I didn't know, after Cleveland, if I'd get another chance. I've learned a lot. A lot on the field, a lot off the field. I'm more flexible now."

And much more successful.

"I think Bill has to be listed with the all-time greats," said Ernie Accorsi, former general manager of the New York Giants. "From George Halas to Paul Brown, Tom Landry, Chuck Noll, Vince Lombardi, Bill Walsh—you have to include him."

Spygate

Spygate wasn't exactly Watergate, but it was similar. Richard Nixon never was going to lose to George McGovern in 1972. So you have to wonder why he had operatives burgle the headquarters of the Democratic National Committee.

And it wasn't as if Bill Belichick, who'd already won three Super Bowls, wasn't going to continue winning his share of games in New England.

Yet, in blatant violation of NFL rules, Belichick instructed one of the team's video assistants, Matt Estrella, to tape the opposing coaches along the sideline as they sent in signals for offensive plays and defensive alignments.

The issue blew up in Belichick's face when his former defensive coordinator Eric Mangini, who then was head coach of the New York Jets, blew the whistle on him at the 2007 season opener at the Meadowlands.

Nor was that the first time the Patriots had done it. The Packers caught them in November 2006 but chose not to turn them in and turn the matter into a cause celebre as the Jets did.

Found guilty as charged, Belichick and the Patriots were punished severely by the NFL. Commissioner Roger Goodell levied a $500,000 fine against Belichick personally, fined the Patriots organization $250,000, and also stripped them of a first-round draft choice in 2008 for what the league office labeled a "calculated and deliberate attempt to avoid long-standing rules designed to encourage fair play and promote honest competition on the playing field."

In other words, Belichick cheated, and he paid a heavy price for it. The fine against him is the largest levied against any coach in NFL history. As for the forfeiture of the first-round choice, never before had the league exacted a No. 1 pick as penalty for a rules transgression. And then there was the blow to Belichick's reputation.

There are few more disparaging, demeaning, and, if the offender has any conscience at all, humiliating and embarrassing labels than "cheater."

It isn't something Belichick is proud of and certainly wasn't something that team owner Robert Kraft, who is understandably protective of his and his franchise's public image, was happy about.

On September 6, 2007—three days before the Pats traveled to New Jersey to take on the Jets—the following memo was sent to NFL coaches and general managers by Ray Anderson, the league's executive vice president of football operations: "Videotaping of any type, including, but not limited to, taping of an opponent's offensive or defensive signals, is prohibited on the sidelines, in the coaches' booth, in the locker room, or at any other locations accessible to club staff members during the game."

Seems pretty straightforward, doesn't it? Perfectly clear and unambiguous, wouldn't you say? Yet what Belichick had to say in the statement he released—but did not read—to the media was, "My interpretation of a rule in the constitution and bylaws was incorrect."

NFL commissioner Roger Goodell addresses the media about Spygate on August 16, 2007. Bill Belichick received the largest fine in NFL history— $500,000—for his role in the videotaping scandal. Photo courtesy of AP Images.

Go back a few paragraphs and read Anderson's memo again. How could that be misinterpreted—especially by a graduate of Wesleyan such as Belichick?

What also was interesting for both Patriots fans and Patriots haters alike was the coach's reluctance—actually, his refusal—to say aloud the words, "I'm sorry. I was wrong. I apologize."

In his written statement, Belichick stated, "I accept full responsibility for the actions that led to [the] ruling. Once again, I apologize to the Kraft family and every person directly or indirectly associated with the New England Patriots for the embarrassment, distraction, and penalty my mistake caused. I also apologize to Patriots fans."

As well he should have. His actions, and by extension those of the New England organization, were shameful, egregious—hence the severe penalty issued by the league—costly, and disappointing.

"There's nothing I can do about the past," Belichick said, clearly eager to put the incident behind him.

But the stigma continued to haunt the Patriots, and, because of the aura of suspicion surrounding the club, made plausible what turned out to be a highly publicized—and also highly erroneous—story published by the *Boston Herald* just before Super Bowl XLII that Belichick had filmed the St. Louis Rams practice in the Louisiana Superdome the day before Super Bowl XXXVI in New Orleans.

In this instance it was the newspaper, not the Patriots, who were embarrassed, because the accusation proved false. But it's hard to say how much of a distraction the story was—the general feeling among those close to the club was that it was not much of one, if any—especially breaking when it did.

Unnecessarily compounding the furor over Spygate just prior to the Super Bowl was publicity-seeking U.S. Senator Arlen Specter, a Republican from the commonwealth of Pennsylvania.

One would think Specter had more pressing problems on his plate with combat ongoing in Iraq and Afghanistan and the economy going down the tubes. Then again, as the late Speaker of the House Tip O'Neill liked to say, "All politics is local."

Not coincidentally, Specter has ties to Comcast, the cable company that was battling the NFL over the airing of games available only on the league's network.

In the end, most reasonable football fans agreed with the commissioner's assessment of how Spygate was handled by the NFL.

"The action we took," Goodell said, "was decisive, and it was unprecedented, and it sent a loud message, not only to the Patriots, but to every NFL team, that you better follow the rules."

Coaching Tree

Bill Belichick's "coaching tree" has been bearing fruit. Unfortunately the taste has been more sour than sweet.

Four of Belichick's former coordinators in New England have gone on to head coaching jobs, the most recent being 33-year-old offensive coordinator Josh McDaniels, who was hired in Denver in 2009 to replace two-time Super Bowl champion Mike Shanahan.

Broncos fans are hoping McDaniels will be more successful than Belichick's other top protégés—Charlie Weis, who has struggled at Notre Dame after getting off to a hot start, and Romeo Crennel and Eric Mangini, who both were fired at the end of 2008 by, respectively, Cleveland and the New York Jets. In a bit of an unusual twist, Mangini then was hired to replace Crennel as coach of the Browns.

Great things were expected of Weis when he returned to his alma mater in 2005. As offensive coordinator in New England, he played an important role in the development of star quarterback Tom Brady, who led the Patriots to three Super Bowl victories in four seasons, twice winning the game's MVP Award.

Notre Dame contacted Weis in early December 2004, with the Patriots on their way to the playoffs and the chance to join the Dallas Cowboys as only the second team in NFL history to win three Super Bowls in the space of four years.

Weis wanted the job of coaching the Fighting Irish. "We're talking about the premier football program in the country," he said. "I had gone to school there. This wasn't just any job." But Weis told Notre Dame he wouldn't leave New England until after the playoffs and that he was expecting the Patriots to go to—and win—another Super Bowl. "I owed it to the Patriots and the people of New England to finish what we started," he said.

While he put the Patriots first, Weis also spent time calling recruits. National Signing Day occurred the week the Pats were in Jacksonville for Super Bowl XXXIX.

"Time management," he said, "is a skill I understand. I'm very proud to say that here we are at the Super Bowl, it's Signing Day, and we're getting the right kids at Notre Dame."

Weis' ability to recruit was a question mark. There never was any doubt about his talent as an offensive mastermind.

"Charlie is a very smart person," Belichick said. "He really understands what defenses are doing and how to attack them. He's an outstanding play-caller and has a great sense of timing of when to call certain plays. It's one thing to put together a game plan, and it's another to call the plays at the right time, when they match up the way you want to match up. It's not an easy thing to do.

"He's very good at making adjustments during a game. He sees when some of the things that we thought were good don't look that good and we need to shift to something else. He is decisive and smart. He can pull the trigger. He's not afraid to make tough decisions or to make calls in critical situations. He knows what he wants to do and he does it with a lot of confidence."

What has been ironic and puzzling is that, while Weis has had two recruiting classes ranked among the top 10, Notre Dame's offense the past two years has been woeful. He got off to a great start in 2005 when he inherited quarterback Brady Quinn, who was a first-round draft choice of Crennel and the Browns in 2007. With Quinn at quarterback, Weis' offensive wizardry was very much in evidence as the Irish—6–6 under Tyrone Willingham in 2004—went 9–2, came within seconds of upsetting Southern Cal, and went to the Fiesta Bowl, where they lost to Ohio State.

Weis took Notre Dame to another BCS bowl in 2006 when Quinn was a senior. The Irish were 10–2, although they were soundly beaten by LSU in the Sugar Bowl. But the future looked bright as Weis signed Jimmy Clausen, a quarterback considered the top recruit in the country. Since then, things have bottomed out.

Clausen was thrust into the lineup as a freshman as the Irish stumbled through one of their worst seasons in history. They were 1–9 before winning their final two games against Duke and Stanford, two weak opponents. Notre Dame even lost to Navy, ending a 43-game winning streak for the Irish that started in 1964. Perhaps even more embarrassing to Weis was that Notre Dame ranked dead last—119 of 119—in the nation in yards gained per game.

Notre Dame wasn't appreciably better in 2008, when they finished 7–6 and again struggled offensively. The Irish couldn't get the ball into the end zone in four overtimes against Pittsburgh and lost at home to the Panthers. They couldn't score a single point in a loss at Boston College and didn't make a first down until the waning minutes of the third quarter in a 38–3 drubbing at Southern Cal. They became the first Notre Dame team ever to lose to a team with eight losses when Syracuse scored two touchdowns in the fourth quarter to come from behind and defeat the Irish 24–23 on Senior Day in South Bend. The 15 losses in 2007–08 were the most in any two-year period in Notre Dame history.

The lone bright spot in an otherwise second straight dismal season was that the Irish finally snapped an NCAA-record losing streak in bowl games, beating Hawaii 49–21 in the Hula Bowl in Honolulu after having dropped nine in a row.

Crennel also left New England after the triumphant 2004 season. He appeared to have the Browns on the right track in 2007 when they finished 10–6 and just missed the playoffs. But they plummeted to 4–12 in 2008, and Crennel got the ax, just one year after having received a contract extension.

He had three losing seasons in Cleveland and a four-year record of 24–40. Not only did he never make the playoffs, but he was 0–8 against the Steelers, the Browns' archrival, and was 5–19 overall against AFC North opponents.

He was replaced by Mangini, whom Belichick may have pruned from his coaching tree in the wake of Spygate. Mangini and Belichick already were at odds because Belichick was angered that Mangini, who replaced Crennel as defensive coordinator in New England, had joined the Jets, a division rival with whom Belichick had parted unpleasantly.

Mangini was fired after just three seasons in New York. The Jets had been 4–12 in 2005, the year before he arrived, and he quickly turned them into a playoff team, going 10–6. They lost in the wild-card round to New England and then slipped back to 4–12 in 2007.

The Jets got off to an 8–3 start in 2008, when Brett Favre came out of a brief retirement to quarterback the team, and appeared to be in control of the AFC East. But they collapsed down the stretch, losing four of their last five games—three of them to nonplayoff teams—and finished 9–7, a nonplayoff team themselves. That got Mangini fired.

Still only 38, he will be fired-up to prove the Jets made a major mistake in cutting him loose and, like Belichick, may be a much better coach the second time around, having learned from painful experience.

Experience is something the youthful McDaniels clearly is lacking, although his credentials as an offensive coordinator are impressive. He was, after all, in charge of the offense that scored an NFL-record 589 points while going 16–0 in 2007 when Tom Brady threw for a league-record 50 touchdowns and Randy Moss caught a league-record 23 touchdown passes. What was almost as impressive—perhaps more so depending on one's point of view—was how, in 2008, McDaniels was able to bring along Matt Cassel, who hadn't started a game since high school, but was thrust into the lineup when Brady was injured in the first quarter of the first game of the season. Although the Pats didn't make the playoffs for the first time since 2002, they finished 11–5 and Cassel played well, getting better and better as the season progressed.

That's encouraging for the fans in Denver. What's discouraging is that Mangini lasted just three years in New York, Crennel was fired after four in Cleveland, and if Weis doesn't have a significantly better season at Notre Dame in 2009 than he's had the previous two years, he could be out of a job, too.

chapter 10

The Golden Boy

We're going to play a little word-association game here. Or, more accurately, a name-association game.

I say: Joe Montana.

You say: Jerry Rice, of course.

I say: Johnny Unitas.

You say: Raymond Berry.

Peyton Manning? Marvin Harrison. Terry Bradshaw? Lynn Swann. Troy Aikman? Michael Irvin.

Okay, we're on a roll.

Now, how about if I say Tom Brady? Do you say Randy Moss? Maybe. More likely, you say Gisele Bundchen. For everyone who suggests Wes Welker, there's another who'll bring up Bridget Moynihan.

That's the way it is for America's cover-boy quarterback, the handsome guy with the accurate arm, dimpled chin, and, oh yes, Cover Girl wife.

Even though Tom has graced the covers of publications ranging from *Sports Illustrated* to *GQ*, from *ESPN the Magazine* to *Esquire*, from *The Sporting News* to the fashion-glossy *VMAN*, he'll never match the cover count of the lovely—make that gorgeous; and, go ahead, may as well add incredibly sexy—Gisele, the Brazilian supermodel with whom he's been pictured everywhere from restaurants in Paris to beaches in Costa Rica to poolside in Puerto Vallarta.

With paparazzi pursuing them more tenaciously than the Giants' pass rushers came after Brady in Super Bowl XLII, the celebrity couple

Tom Brady and model Gisele Bundchen depart from the Metropolitan Museum of Art Costume Institute Gala, Superheroes: Fashion and Fantasy, *held at the Metropolitan Museum of Art on May 5, 2008 in New York City.*

has been photographed on the streets of Manhattan and Beverly Hills, at a glamorous gala at the Metropolitan Museum of Art in New York, and serving Thanksgiving dinner at the distinctly unglamorous Goodwill headquarters in Boston.

Gisele is not someone Brady is eager to talk about. Indeed, when *Esquire* asked to interview the superstar quarterback for an article to accompany his presence on the cover of the September 2008 issue, an audience with "the Brady"—as the writer referred to him—was granted on the condition that neither Ms. Bundchen nor Brady's young son, whose mother is actress Bridget Moynihan, are discussed.

If they are, the interviewer is informed by one of Brady's handlers, the offending writer will be dropped "on the f*cking 405."

Well, okay then.

Once upon a time—back when he was a rookie sixth-round draft choice and listed fourth on the depth chart of the New England Patriots—Brady was a most accessible, most congenial, most pleasant, articulate, humble, and entirely likeable young man.

Those were the days when he had trouble convincing skeptics at a local health club that he did, indeed, play for the Patriots. Those also were the days he was trying to convince the skeptics in the New England organization that he should, indeed, be playing for them.

If the personnel experts in the NFL had thought Brady was all that good, coming out of the University of Michigan in 2000, he wouldn't have still been available in the sixth round on draft day.

Brady's day had been spoiled much earlier, when his hometown 49ers—the team he'd rooted for as a kid growing up in San Mateo, the team he'd dreamed of playing for someday—ignored his availability early in Round 3 to draft Giovanni Carmazzi of Hofstra. Giovanni Carmazzi? Of Hofstra, for crying out loud!

"I loved the 49ers," said Brady, whose father, also named Tom, had season tickets and would take young Tommy to Niners games at Candlestick Park. "That's when I realized I wanted to be a football player, going to all those games growing up. I had posters of Joe Montana and Jerry Rice on my walls.

Tom Brady passes against the Tampa Bay Buccaneers during a game on December 18, 2005. Photo courtesy of AP Images.

"I remember sitting in my living room as the 49ers were drafting that day and seeing them pick a quarterback in the third round. I was so mad."

His disposition didn't improve as the rounds continued to roll by and his phone still didn't ring. He remained a wallflower at the draft dance as the Ravens took Chris Redman out of Louisville, the Steelers chose Tee Martin of Tennessee, and the Browns selected Spergon Wynn out of Southwest Texas State.

Spergon Wynn? Southwest Texas State? That may have been even a bigger blow to Brady's pride than the 49ers taking the guy from Hofstra.

The Patriots finally took Brady with the 199th overall selection, after they'd already picked defensive back Antwan Harris earlier in Round 6. Clearly they were in no rush to pick Brady, having taken a tight end out of Boise State named Dave Stachelski along with Jeff Marriott, a defensive tackle from Missouri, in Round 5.

"I'll never forget that day," Brady said.

The reason he lasted so long, said Scott Pioli, who's now running the football operation for the Chiefs in Kansas City, but then was in charge of the draft in New England, was that, "People were apprehensive about his arm strength and overall body bulk. Some people felt he was too skinny and that he was a marginal athlete."

There also was some concern because Brady battled for the starting job at Michigan with Drew Henson. Not surprisingly, some scouts wondered if he could be a starter in the NFL if he hadn't been the clear-cut No. 1 for the Wolverines.

Yet it was how Brady dealt with the controversy over his situation in Ann Arbor that impressed Pioli and the Patriots.

"He handled it like a man," Pioli said. "It's so cliché to say, but drafting players is an inexact science. It's not always about height, weight, and speed. It's not always about arm strength and athleticism. It's a total package. We liked Tom's leadership and the maturity he showed."

Brady arrived in New England determined to show the Patriots they'd made the best draft pick in franchise history.

"Tommy came in with a little bit of a chip on his shoulder," said Charlie Weis, then the Patriots offensive coordinator and now head coach at Notre Dame. "Robert Kraft told me later that Tommy had told him he was going to prove to be the best draft pick the Patriots ever made."

In the nine seasons since, Brady has certainly made his case. He's taken the Patriots to four Super Bowls, won three of them—it would have been all four had the New England defense not allowed the Giants to drive 83 yards to the winning touchdown in the final three minutes of Super Bowl XLII—and was named Most Valuable Player in two. And, prior to the 2007 season, he'd done it all despite having receivers who don't begin to compare with the likes of Rice, Berry, Harrison, Swann, or Irvin.

Brady's leading receiver in 2001, when the Patriots won their first Super Bowl, was Troy Brown. In 2003 it was Deion Branch. In 2004, David Givens. In 2006, when it was another last-minute defensive letdown that allowed the Colts to come from behind and keep New England from going to the Super Bowl, Brady's go-to guy was Reche Caldwell, who wasn't wanted in San Diego and couldn't start in Washington.

When the Patriots finally got Brady some top-quality pass-catchers, signing Moss and trading for Welker in 2007, he displayed his gratitude and his considerable talents by throwing for an NFL-record 50 touchdowns as the Patriots put up 589 points—an average of 37 per game— and went undefeated, a perfect 16–0, during the regular season.

Not that he hadn't long before established his credentials as a bona fide superstar. If he hadn't done it by leading the Patriots to a stunning upset of the St. Louis Rams in Super Bowl XXXVI, he certainly did it by winning another championship—and another MVP award—two years later when the Pats beat the Panthers in Super Bowl XXXVIII. Adding another Lombardi Trophy the following season, when the Patriots knocked off the Eagles in Super Bowl XXXIX, was icing on the cake.

By then Brady was a full-fledged Celebrity, with a capital C. He'd had an audience with Pope John Paul II at the Vatican. "It's the most nervous I've ever been meeting anyone in my life," Brady said. "It was an incredible experience, one I'll never forget." He's also mingled with the lovelies at Hugh Hefner's Playboy mansion, where presumably he wasn't so nervous.

As no less an authority than Donald Trump observed on the occasion of the Miss USA 2002 pageant, at which he and Brady were judges, "The kid has great self-confidence and an unbelievable personality, and he's got the maturity of a much older man. Let me tell you, if one thing stands out about Tom Brady, it's that he loves those women. And, guess what? They love him, too."

What's not to love? In addition to being a Hall of Fame–caliber NFL quarterback, Brady is as handsome as he is talented. And charming, and articulate, and considerate, and, well, the list could go on and on. The point is, he has the arm and poise to get the game ball and the looks and charm to get the girl.

Not only has Brady been *Sports Illustrated*'s Sportsman of the Year, but he's also topped *Esquire*'s list of best-dressed men and is considered an "icon of cool," by *GQ*, which featured him on the cover of its 50th anniversary issue. Which is, everyone can probably agree, pretty cool, indeed.

But, if you're a Patriots fan, that also may be something that's troubling you just a little bit. Or, perhaps, more than a little bit.

Because, after never missing a start since stepping in for the injured Drew Bledsoe in the second game of the 2001 season—racking up a string of 128 in a row, including playoff games—Brady lasted only through the first half of the first quarter of the first game of the 2008 season. That's when, in the season opener in Foxboro against the lowly Chiefs, he suffered torn knee ligaments that sidelined him for the rest of the year.

Since then he's been seen but rarely heard from. The paparazzi provided pictures aplenty, but Brady's words were few and far between. Claiming he didn't want to be a "distraction," he wasn't on hand to support his teammates on game days. An infection following his surgery resulted in a setback to his rehab, setting rumors flying about whether he'd be ready for the 2009 opener.

A hard worker throughout his career—the summer after winning his first Super Bowl, Brady was awarded a prime parking spot at training camp for his diligence during off-season workouts—the allure of the weight room may pale these days when compared to the other opportunities in Brady's glamorous life.

Part of his success has been due to his ability, despite his ever-growing celebrity and the adulation he receives from fans both male and female, to remain "one of the guys" in the New England locker room.

"You never want to lose the respect of the guys you play with," he said, "because that's everything. I don't need to be the showstopper. I'd much rather people assume I'm one of the guys."

His teammates—and his opponents—certainly respect what Brady does on the field.

"The most obvious thing about him—and the best thing about him—is that he wins," said Troy Polamalu, the hard-hitting All-Pro safety for the Super Bowl champion Steelers.

"Tom is a winner," Belichick concurs. "A quarterback's job is to do what he needs to do to make the team win. Tom does that as well as anybody."

Like other all-time greats such as Johnny Unitas and Joe Montana, in whose Hall of Fame company he clearly belongs, Brady is at his best in the biggest games. When the pressure's highest, he's at his coolest.

"What really makes him special," said Brown, "is how he stays cool under pressure. He's been able to make big plays in key situations. When you can make those plays, you win big games."

"He's the main reason," Branch said, "why everyone else on the team stays calm in tight situations."

Brady was so calm prior to his first Super Bowl that he dozed off in the New England locker room.

"I was laying on the floor and just fell asleep," he said. "When I woke up, I didn't think I would feel as good as I felt. You always think, *I'd be so nervous in the Super Bowl.* But that's when I feel best, because I feel like I'm most prepared."

Brady always has worked hard to prepare for games. "There's nobody," said Patriots left tackle Matt Light, "that prepares better than Tommy. I've never been around a guy who takes each moment of practice as seriously as he does. It comes down to a great work ethic. Every game means a lot to him. He leads by example. It helps you pick your own game up a notch. Every game, you're playing for perfection. That's what he's doing, and it trickles down to everybody else on the team."

Prior to playing the Eagles in Super Bowl XXXIX in Jacksonville, Brady was continually knocking on Weis' hotel room door at all hours of the day and night.

"He kept asking, 'Can we add this? Can we drop this? He was a pain in the butt, really," Weis said. "I finally said to him, 'Can you give me a break and let me get some sleep?'"

Weis has a special relationship with Brady, stemming from when Weis almost died from complications following gastric bypass surgery in the summer of 2002.

As Weis wrote in his book, *No Excuses*, "Tommy was the one person who was there through that whole ordeal. During rookie camp, which rookies and all of the quarterbacks attend for about a week before the full squad arrives for the start of regular training camp, he would finish up with the quarterback meeting at night and then drive over to my house to perk me up. My wife [Maura] would say to me that the only part of the day when I tried to gather myself up to not act like I was sick was when he came over. Tommy would just sit and talk with me before going back to camp in time for bed check. We'd talk football, but we'd talk about everything else, too. It wasn't just that he took the time to come over to see me. He genuinely cared. I feel forever indebted to Tommy."

Brady has made it a point to remain genuine, to keep it real and not get caught up in his celebrity or the hype that surrounds him both on and off the field. His teammates—especially the offensive linemen who block for him—are only too happy to help him in that regard.

In 2005 Brady did a photo shoot for *GQ* that included a picture of him holding a goat. The day the magazine hit the stands, Brady walked up to the line of scrimmage at practice and there, staring up at him as he stood behind the line prepared to take the snap, was the page picturing him and the goat, displayed on the backs of light and center Dan Koppen. Everyone started laughing, no one harder than Brady.

"Tom goes through so much," Koppen says. "I don't know how I would deal with that stuff."

Among the "stuff" that is part of Brady's everyday life is playing in the Pebble Beach National Pro-Am, visiting the White House, riding with Mickey Mouse at Disneyland after winning the Super Bowl, throwing out the first ball at Fenway Park, endorsing Movado watches and

Stetson cologne, and filming television commercials such as the one for a credit-card company in which he included all of his offensive linemen.

That, too, was a part of trying to remain "one of the guys." But how can Brady really be one of the guys when the mother of his child is a Hollywood actress and his wife is a sultry Brazilian supermodel who has graced more magazine covers than any woman this side of the late Princess Diana?

"Regular guys" don't jet-set from Paris to Cabo, Costa Rica to the West Coast, Manhattan to the fashion runways of Milan.

Brady turns 32 in the summer of 2009. He's no longer the fresh-faced kid who, in the heady moments after Adam Vinatieri's field goal sailed through the uprights to upset the Rams in Super Bowl XXXVI, grabbed Drew Bledsoe, the guy he'd replaced, and shouted, "We won! Can you believe it? We f*cking won!"

He's won two more titles since then and would have had a fourth—as well as a perfect 19–0 season, a permanent piece of NFL history—had the New England defense been able to stop the Giants

Instead of displaying boyish enthusiasm, Brady now sports stylish stubble and looks stunning in Zegna suits. He poses wearing a wet T-shirt for *VMAN*. He is, as *GQ* declared, "an icon of cool."

The Patriots insist they're cool with that. "Among the reasons Tom's successful," Belichick said "are because he's resilient, he's tough-minded, he's a quick thinker, a hard worker, an accurate passer. He's also charismatic, with outstanding leadership qualities.

"There's hardly anything you can criticize the guy for. He works hard. He treats every teammate with respect. He doesn't expect anything that everyone else doesn't get, too."

But Brady isn't like everyone, as much he tries to be.

"One thing you realize when you play a team sport," he said, "is that everybody, not just one guy, is responsible for any success you may have. I don't think I've ever lost sight of that. The reasons we've been successful in New England are because of a lot of sacrifice, a lot of hard work, by a lot of people. It's certainly not a one-man band. I feel lucky to be a part of it."

The Patriots certainly are lucky to have him. And, you know what? Gisele probably feels the same way.

chapter 11

Robert Kraft

The aluminum bench on which the family of Robert Kraft used to sit when he first bought season tickets to Patriots games in Foxboro (an expense that his wife, Myra, did not think was necessary) now sits unobtrusively on the second floor of the Patriots Hall of Fame. Section 217, Row 25, down near the 10-yard line. That's where the Family Kraft sat in the old stadium.

The owner's suite. That's where the Family Kraft sits now in Gillette Stadium, the 68,756-seat pigskin palace that cost $325 million, just about all of that put up by Robert Kraft himself.

The stadium, which opened in 2002, is quite a sight to see, although it's not that easy to see anymore, tucked as it is amidst the sprawling Bass Pro Shop, the Brigham and Women's/Mass General Health Care Center, the CBS Scene restaurant and bar, and a number of other retail outlets and dining establishments, not to mention—coming soon!—a Marriott Renaissance hotel.

A renaissance doesn't begin to describe what has taken place on the site of what was, before pro football came to Foxboro, a harness-racing track. None of what the football fan, hungry wayfarer, or eager shopper sees now would be here if not for Robert Kraft.

Of course, the Patriots wouldn't be here, either, if it weren't for Robert Kraft. The franchise appeared headed for St. Louis in 1994, about to be delivered to the city that had lost the football Cardinals to Arizona by James Busch (as in beer) Orthwein, who had bought the Patriots from Remington razor magnate Victor Kiam in 1992.

"The team was gone if somebody didn't step up with a good local bid," Kraft said. Up stepped Kraft, who had begun to position himself to buy the team as far back as 1985. Billy Sullivan had the family business on the market. Kraft, who had built his father-in-law's business—the Rand-Whitney Group of Worcester, Massachusetts—into one of the largest privately owned paper and packaging companies in the United States, was interested in buying.

Spurned by Sullivan, Kraft settled for purchasing an option to buy the land around the stadium. Three years later, with the stadium burdened by debt and mired in bankruptcy court, Kraft outbid Kiam for the facility and, more importantly, the lease that required the Patriots to play in it.

"As in any business," Kraft said, "you're always trying to figure how to get a competitive edge. That option was the first step that allowed me to have an edge. We wound up controlling the parking for all the events at the stadium. We overpaid [$1 million a year for 10 years] in order to have the right to one day buy the team."

Kiam couldn't understand why anyone would buy the stadium if they didn't own the team, so he submitted a low bid to the bankruptcy court. Kraft's bankers felt much the same way.

"My bankers," he said, "thought I was nuts, that I was buying a white elephant, that the team would never play there. But the bankruptcy judge reaffirmed our lease on the stadium through 2001, which turned out to be the year we won the Super Bowl."

Kraft paid $22 million for the stadium. The lease in his pocket was also his ace in the hole in his high-stakes gamble to buy the team. According to the terms of the lease, if the Patriots were going to play anywhere, it had to be in Foxboro or else payment of treble damages would be awarded to the stadium owner.

When St. Louis was not awarded an expansion franchise, Kraft was offered $75 million to break the lease, which would allow Orthwein to move the team.

"My wife wanted me to take it," Kraft said. Not only was Kraft an ardent football fan and a shrewd businessman, but he also had been a fan of the Boston Braves, the National League baseball team that had broken his young heart when they left town for Milwaukee in 1953.

Patriots owner Robert Kraft holds up the Lombardi trophy after the Patriots defeated the Philadelphia Eagles 24–21 in Super Bowl XXXIX at Alltel Stadium in Jacksonville, Florida, on February 6, 2005.

"A part of me died when the Braves left," said Kraft, who grew up in Brookline, an affluent suburb of Boston. "I regret that to this day. They were my team."

Instead of pocketing a hefty profit, Kraft wound up spending $172 million—then the highest price ever paid for an NFL franchise—to purchase the Patriots.

"At Harvard Business School," said Kraft, who earned a master's degree there after graduating from Columbia, where he had been a running back on the lightweight football team, "they teach you to buy low and sell high. We broke that rule. But this was a unique opportunity. I realized it would likely be the only chance in my lifetime to do something like this."

That memory of the Braves' departure also played a part in Kraft's decision several years later, in 1999, when he was offered a deal he seemingly couldn't refuse to move the Patriots to Hartford, Connecticut.

He wanted a new stadium. But it had become apparent that if he wanted to build it in Massachusetts, he was going to have to do it with his own money. The politicians of the Nutmeg State, however, were not only willing to use public funds to pay for a new stadium for the Patriots but also were prepared to guarantee that the team's revenues would rank among the top three in the league for 30 years with any shortfall from the sale of tickets and luxury suites to be made up by the state.

"We had a family meeting," Kraft said. "Five members voted that we stay in Foxboro. One said Connecticut." That one was Kraft's oldest son, Jonathan, a Williams College grad who, like his father, earned his M.B.A. at Harvard Business School.

"Dad," he said, "you just broke every rule of finance." Kraft knew Jonathan was right about that, but he also knew in his heart that he was doing the right thing by keeping the team in greater Boston.

"Instead of accepting a deal that would have cost us nothing," Robert Kraft said, "we went into debt for over $300 million to build our own stadium. It was a dumb financial move. But it just felt like the right thing.

"You know, some things in life aren't about cash-flow statements. The decision wasn't based on money. I knew I'd feel better having a stadium close to home. I knew we'd find a way to make it work.

"We built this stadium with the fans in mind. I remember sitting on that aluminum bench in the old stadium freezing my buns off. This stadium, and our championship teams, are my family's legacy to this region."

chapter 12

Drafts

Let's call this a Dream Draft, the best of the best. The 2009 draft was the 50th in franchise history for the New England Patriots. Here's a look at the best picks ever made in each round over the past half-century.

Round 1

1a: John Hannah, OG, 1973

Considered one of the best—some would say *the* best—offensive linemen in NFL history, this Hall of Fame guard ranks as the best first-round pick in Patriots history.

1b: Mike Haynes, CB, 1976

Also a member of the Pro Football Hall of Fame, Haynes ranks among the top corners ever to play the game.

1c: Drew Bledsoe, QB, 1993

Along with Bill Parcells, he came to New England in 1993 and returned the Patriots to respectability. The first player taken that year in the entire draft—the Pats had gone 2–14 in 1992, after having been 1–15 in 1990—Bledsoe took them to the playoffs in 1994 and to the Super Bowl in 1996. He also made playoff appearances in 1997 and 1998, when Pete Carroll was coach, and came off the bench in the 2001 AFC championship in Pittsburgh when Tom Brady was injured and threw a touchdown pass that helped put the Patriots in the Super Bowl. His performance against Minnesota in 1994 when he completed 45 of 70 passes—both NFL records—for a club-record 426 yards and three touchdowns without throwing a single interception ranks as one of the all-time best, not just in team history but in league history. In that game he rallied the Patriots from a 20–0 deficit to a 26–20 overtime victory.

1d: Bruce Armstrong (1987), a six-time Pro Bowl selection at left tackle who holds the club record for games played (212) also deserves a mention.

Best First Round Ever: 1973.

In addition to Hannah, who was taken fourth overall, the Patriots also selected RB Sam Cunningham (11) and WR Darryl Stingley (19).

Round 2

Andre Tippett, LB, 1982

A fearsome pass rusher, Tippett joined Hannah and Haynes in the Hall of Fame in 2008. He is the Patriots' all-time sacks leader with 100—well ahead of the next man on the list, defensive end Julius Adams, who had 79.5 from 1971 through 1987. Almost unblockable, Tippett set a franchise season record for sacks in 1984 with 18.5 and had 16.5 in 1985.

Round 3

Tedy Bruschi, LB, 1996

One of the more popular players the Patriots have ever had, Bruschi has been to five Super Bowls, more than any player in team history. Next-best at No. 3 is running back Curtis Martin (1995).

Round 4

Asante Samuel, DB, 2003

Samuel had a total of 16 interceptions in 2006–07 but failed to come down with the one that could have clinched Super Bowl XLII and preserved a perfect 19–0 season. Pats fans irritated by that may opt for linebacker Don Blackmon (1981) at this spot.

Round 5

Ben Coates, TE, 1991

Bledsoe's go-to guy, Coates was the Patriots' leading receiver for five of six seasons from 1993 through 1998, including a career-high 96 catches in 1994. He was elected to the team's Hall of Fame in 2008.

Another notable fifth-rounder was free safety Fred Marion (1982), who had a team-high seven interceptions when the Pats won the AFC championship in 1985 and went to the Super Bowl for the first time.

Round 6

Tom Brady, QB, 2000

The single-best pick in Patriots history, especially considering the value. Heck, with two Super Bowl MVP awards, he'd have been the single-best pick in Patriots history if he'd been a first-rounder. It's hard to believe he wasn't taken earlier, but he wasn't even the Pats' first pick in Round 6 in 2000. They selected cornerback Antwan Harris at No. 187 overall. Brady didn't go until No. 199.

Round 7

Craig James, RB, 1983

A star at Southern Methodist, where he teamed with Eric Dickerson in the Mustangs' famed Pony Express backfield, James was playing for the Washington Federals of the USFL when the Pats picked him in 1983. He came to New England the following year and, in the Super Bowl season of 1985, led the team in rushing with 1,227 yards on 263 carries.

Round 8

Troy Brown, WR, 1993

Cut in 1994 by Parcells, who had drafted him the year before, Brown returned to the Patriots later that season and went on to become the team's all-time receiving leader. He also has returned more punts for more yards than any player in team history. As if that weren't enough, when injuries decimated the New England secondary in 2004, Brown filled in at defensive back and made three interceptions, helping the Pats win their third Super Bowl in four years.

It's too bad the draft no longer lasts eight rounds because, in addition to Brown, the Pats have picked up the likes of fullback Sam Gash (1992), defensive back Ronnie Lippett (1983), and tight end Lin Dawson (1981) in the eighth round.

Round 9

John Spagnola, TE, 1979

He played 10 years in the NFL. Unfortunately, none of them were for the Patriots, who had Russ Francis and Don Hasselbeck when they selected Spagnola out of Yale.

Round 10
Toby Williams, DL, 1983

    Irving Fryar's teammate at Nebraska, Williams started 56 games for the Patriots through the 1988 season.

Round 11
Marvin Allen, RB, 1988

    Not only did Allen average four yards per carry on 94 rushing attempts as well as return kickoffs for the Pats over four seasons, but he also has been one of the team's top scouts since 1997.

Round 12 and Above
A Hall of Famer in the 13th round—how's that for value? That's when the Patriots plucked linebacker Nick Buoniconti out of Notre Dame in 1962. He wasn't drafted at all by the NFL because he was thought to be too small at 5'11" and 220 pounds. But toughness, intelligence, and heart aren't measurable, and Buoniconti went on to become a five-time AFL All-Star for the Pats before being traded to Miami, where he was a big name on the Dolphins' No Name Defense that won back-to-back Super Bowls and put together a perfect season in 1972, going 17–0.

Busts
We've examined the best drafts in Patriots history, but what about the worst? Here are the five biggest busts, in order of the year of their selection.

    Dennis Byrd, DL, 1968—A great college player at North Carolina State, where he was a two-time All-American, Byrd was the sixth player drafted overall, even though he'd suffered a serious knee injury late in his senior season. He never really recovered and played just one season for the Patriots. "I don't think I was ever the same [after the injury]," Byrd said. Obviously, he wasn't.

    Hart Lee Dykes, WR, 1989—A marvelous athlete who also excelled in basketball and baseball in high school in Bay City, Texas, he was the object of a college recruiting battle that resulted in four schools—Texas A&M, Oklahoma, Illinois, and Oklahoma State (where he finally ended up)—being placed on probation by the NCAA. He lasted just two seasons in New England, his career brought to an abrupt and disappointing end by a broken kneecap and also because he had vision problems stemming from when he and Irving Fryar were involved in a late-night bar fight in 1990.

Dykes is best remembered in New England for a comment he made at his first press conference, just after he was drafted 16ᵗʰ overall. Showing up in Foxboro wearing a tailored suit and a collarless dress shirt, he was complimented by the media on his appearance.

"When you looks good," Dykes said, "you feels good. And when you feels good, you plays good."

Chris Singleton, LB, 1990—Drafted eighth overall out of Arizona, Singleton looked like Tarzan but played like Jane. Running back Emmit Smith was drafted 17ᵗʰ overall that year by the Dallas Cowboys. The Patriots also had the 10ᵗʰ overall pick in the 1990 draft and used it to take defensive lineman Ray Agnew. Singleton spent three-plus seasons with the Patriots and three-plus more with Miami, none of them memorable.

Eugene Chung, OL, 1992—Drafted 13ᵗʰ overall, Chung lasted less than three full seasons in New England. He played a year in Jacksonville and another in Indianapolis but never started a game for either of those teams.

Chris Canty, DB, 1997—The 29ᵗʰ overall pick, Canty is best remembered in New England for being found by North Attleboro police asleep in his car behind a gas station in the wee hours of the morning with an open container of alcohol on the seat beside him. The question asked about his coverage ability was, "Can he? Or Canty?" He couldn't, which is why he lasted only two seasons with the Patriots.

Bonus Picks

Now that we've looked at the best and the worst of Patriots' draft choices, here are a few bonus picks.

Best Draft Day Trade: That's easy. It was in 2007, when the Patriots picked up record-setting wide receiver Randy Moss from the Raiders for a fourth-round choice.

Worst Draft Day Trade: Also easy. It was in 1985, when the Patriots traded their first-round pick, 16ᵗʰ overall, to San Francisco for the 49ers' No. 1 (28ᵗʰ overall) and No. 2 (56ᵗʰ) picks. The Patriots wound up with offensive lineman Trevor Matich and defensive lineman Ben Thomas. The 49ers used that 16th pick to take a wide receiver out of Mississippi Valley State by the name of Jerry Rice.

Best Overall Draft in Club History: This is not so easy. It could have been in 1973, when they landed Hannah, Cunningham, Stingley, and—in the 14th round—nose tackle Ray "Sugar Bear" Hamilton. But it may have been in 1976, when they drafted Haynes, Pete Brock, and Tim Fox—all in the first round—and defensive back Doug Beaudoin in the ninth.

Honorable mention goes to the bountiful crop of 1982—Kenneth Sims, Lester Williams, Robert Weathers, Andre Tippett, Darryl Haley, Cedric Jones, Clayton Weishuhn, George Crump, Brian Ingram, and Fred Marion.

chapter 13

Super Bowl XXXVI

"We shocked the world."

—Lawyer Milloy

"We shocked the world, but we didn't shock ourselves."

—Adam Vinatieri

Even the most ardent Patriots fans would have been shocked if they'd been told, as they walked out of Foxboro Stadium the night of November 18, 2001, after watching the Rams roll to a 24–17 victory, that the Pats wouldn't lose another game the rest of the season and would win the first Super Bowl in franchise history by upsetting that same St. Louis team.

At that point Patriots fans were, if not exactly shocked, at least somewhat surprised their team was even playing .500 ball at 5–5.

It had seemed the season would be lost when quarterback Drew Bledsoe—the face of the franchise since being selected with the first overall pick in the 1993 draft—was seriously injured in the second game, when Jets linebacker Mo Lewis drove his helmet into Bledsoe's chest as the quarterback was trying to get out of bounds in front of the New England bench.

"He got crushed," Charlie Weis, who was the Patriots' offensive coordinator, wrote in his book, *No Excuses*. "It was tense after the game in the trainer's room. The hit on Bledsoe was so hard that it sheared a blood vessel in his chest. His chest cavity started filling with blood, and he was taken to the hospital. Anytime you have internal bleeding, there are potential problems, and he was having some. We're talking life and death. Thankfully, we got that fixed, but he was going to be out for a while."

And who would come in to replace him? Young Tommy Brady, a sixth-round draft choice the previous year out of the University of Michigan, where he'd battled Drew Henson for the starting job.

Brady had played in only one game his rookie year, throwing just three passes (completing one) late in a 34–9 loss to the Lions on Thanksgiving Day in Detroit. But Bill Belichick—and Weis—had been watching him develop in practice. They'd seen a lot they liked in Brady, both on and off the field.

"You could see," Weis said, "that Tommy had something special about him."

Brady played better than most people expected, leading the Patriots to five wins in eight games after they'd lost their first two with Bledsoe. But he had some rough outings, too. He was intercepted four times in the fourth quarter in a loss at Denver. In a win over the Bills the week before the Rams game, he was sacked seven times, threw an interception, passed for just 107 yards, and coughed up what could have been a costly fumble in the fourth quarter. He was sacked four times in a loss at Miami.

He'd certainly looked promising but not exactly special. So when Bledsoe was declared fully healthy and ready to play a few days after the loss to St. Louis, there was no shortage of people in New England who figured he'd start the following Sunday against the Saints. Bledsoe, as expected, was one of those people. But Belichick had other ideas.

"Drew hasn't been able to play the last eight weeks," the coach explained. "Tom's more game-ready. That's the way we're going to go. This isn't about Drew losing a job or being beat out. It's strictly about the team."

Steve Grogan, who'd lost his starting job to young Tony Eason in 1984, could identify with Bledsoe.

"It's fun to see a young guy come off the bench and play the way Brady's played," Grogan said. "But I've also been in Bledsoe's shoes, so I know where he's coming from. He wants to be on the field. It's hard to have someone tell you that you're not the best.

"Drew's situation is different from mine. He got hurt. I got yanked. I didn't see it coming. It was upsetting.

"It's an unwritten rule in the NFL," Grogan continued, "that you don't lose your job to injury. But if you're out a long time and the other guy's playing well, that weighs heavily in the coach's decision. The other thing to keep in mind is that Drew wasn't playing well at the end of last year or in the first couple of games this year. In my opinion, he had gotten locked in a little too much to trying to get the ball downfield. As a result, he was holding it too long."

Questionable at the time—and controversial, too—Belichick's decision to stay with Brady turned out to be brilliant, as the Patriots rolled through the remainder of the regular season, winning their last six games to finish 11–5, good for first place in the AFC East.

After slipping past the Raiders in the Snow Bowl in the conference semifinals, the Patriots went to Pittsburgh and surprised the Steelers, as

Patriots cornerback Ty Law (No. 24) steps in front of St. Louis Rams wide receiver Isaac Bruce (No. 80) and returns a pass 47 yards for a touchdown during Super Bowl XXXVI on February 3, 2002, a 20–17 Pats victory at the Louisiana Superdome.

Bledsoe came off the bench and led the team to victory after Brady twisted a knee in the second quarter.

Naturally Bledsoe hoped to start in the Super Bowl, as he had five years earlier. But Brady was ready to go, and he was the guy Belichick wanted to go with.

"That was the one time Drew was mad at me," Weis wrote, "and at a lot of other people. I could understand why he would be. But with Tommy at quarterback, we had team chemistry going for us."

By the time they took on the heavily favored Rams in Super Bowl XXXVI, the 2001 Patriots could have won a Nobel Prize for Team Chemistry. They truly had become a team, in the best sense of the word, and provided dramatic—and moving—evidence of that in pregame introductions at the Superdome.

The Rams came out first, and they came out individually—each highly touted offensive player getting his "props" and his face time on international television, taking a bow as part of the first offense in NFL history to score more than 500 points in three consecutive seasons. Wide receiver Torry Holt came running out without his helmet on. Running back Marshall Faulk came out bouncing. Quarterback Kurt Warner came out pointing to the roof.

When it was time for the Patriots' defense to be introduced, the entire New England team came out together. The voice of Pat Summerall boomed over the P.A. system, "Choosing to be introduced as a team, the American Football Conference champion New England Patriots." That should have been the Rams' first clue that they were going to have their hands full.

Tom Jackson, the ESPN analyst and former star linebacker for the Denver Broncos, felt then that the upstart Patriots had a great chance of upsetting the high-scoring Rams.

"One of my favorite moments in Super Bowl history," Jackson said, "was when the Patriots were introduced as a team. There aren't many moments when the hair on the back of your neck actually stands up. But when the Patriots came out as a team for pregame introductions, that was one of those moments.

"Everybody wants to be introduced individually at the Super Bowl. I thought right then, even though the Patriots were big underdogs, that they had a good chance to win because they had a mind-set going for them that the Rams didn't have."

The Patriots had only one thing in mind—winning. "It's a great group of guys who are very selfless, just committed to winning," said Brady. "Guys that work hard, respect their coaches, and listen to them. We get out on the field and we all have the same thing in mind. It's fun to lead a group of guys who have no other agenda but winning games."

It's an old cliché that defense wins championships, and, for the first three quarters against the Rams, it seemed to be holding true once again. It was the New England defense that put the first points on the board for the Patriots, cornerback Ty Law intercepting a Warner pass and returning it 47 yards for a touchdown and a 7–3 lead in the second quarter. Two more turnovers enabled New England to extend its lead to 17–3 by the end of the third quarter. A fumble recovery led to an eight-yard touchdown pass from Brady to David Patten just before halftime, and an interception by Otis Smith set up a 37-yard field goal by Adam Vinatieri.

But the St. Louis offense didn't get its billing as "the Greatest Show on Turf" for no reason. Warner brought the Rams back in the fourth quarter, scoring himself on a two-yard run that cut New England's lead to 17–10, then throwing a 26-yard touchdown pass to Ricky Proehl that tied the game with just 1:30 left.

When the Patriots, who had no timeouts remaining, returned the ensuing kickoff only to the 17, it seemed overtime was imminent—which didn't bode well for the Pats, considering that the Rams appeared to have all the momentum.

It was because the Rams were rolling that Weis felt the Patriots should try to win in regulation. Belichick was more conservative, wanting to pick up a first down before making an all-out effort to get the ball downfield.

Before Brady trotted out on the field, Weis cautioned him to "take care of the football."

After which, Bledsoe grabbed Brady and said, "F*ck that. Go out there and sling it."

As it turned out, Brady took both seemingly contrary pieces of advice to heart. A couple of quick, short tosses to running back J.R.

Redmond put the Pats on their own 30, where Brady spiked the ball to stop the clock with 41 seconds left. He then threw again to Redmond, who was able to get of bounds after gaining 11 yards.

Following an incompletion, and with the St. Louis secondary guarding against the deep ball, Brady threw underneath the coverage to his favorite receiver, Troy Brown, who'd set a team record that season by making 101 catches. The play was good for 23 yards to the Rams' 36, where Brown stopped the clock with 21 seconds to go by running out of bounds.

Weis directed Brady to dump a short toss to tight end Jerome Wiggins in order to get Vinatieri a bit closer and emphasized to his young quarterback that he should be sure everyone knew to get quickly to the line of scrimmage after the play so he could spike the ball. Brady threw for a quick six yards and then was able to stop the clock with seven seconds remaining.

"I was just so happy," Vinatieri said, "that the guys moved the ball down and gave me a chance to kick."

The Patriots knew there was no chance Vinatieri was going to miss the kick. For one thing, he'd never missed indoors in his career. For another, if he made those field goals in the snow to beat the Raiders, there was no way he wasn't going to put the ball squarely through the uprights from 48 yards in the climate-controlled conditions of the Superdome. "Once I kicked it," he said, "I knew it was good. I looked up, and it was time to celebrate."

chapter 14

Super Bowl XXXVIII

The Patriots had won 14 in a row as they prepared to play the Carolina Panthers in Super Bowl XXXVIII in Houston.

They'd gotten off to a slow start in 2003, going 2–2 after missing the playoffs the year before, when they'd followed up their 2001 championship season by slipping to 9–7. Then, just as they had in 2001, when they won their last nine games and capped a remarkable season with a 20–17 upset of St. Louis in Super Bowl XXXVI, the Patriots got on a roll.

"To win 14 in a row—that's unbelievable," quarterback Tom Brady said.

What made it even more unbelievable is that the Patriots did it despite a wave of injuries that resulted in a league-high 87 games missed by starters.

"Who does that?" Brady said of the winning streak his team was taking into the Super Bowl. "To do that takes great will, great preparation, and great execution. But if we don't win 15, our goal hasn't been achieved."

There never is any question about what the goal is for Bill Belichick's Patriots teams: Win the Super Bowl.

The Pats advanced to their second Super Bowl in three seasons by beating the high-scoring Indianapolis Colts 24–14 in the AFC Championship Game in Foxboro. The key statistic in the game was that Patriots cornerback Ty Law had as many interceptions—three—as Marvin Harrison, the Colts' All-Pro wide receiver, had receptions. While Law returned his interceptions 26 yards, Harrison was held to a mere 19 yards.

New England's defensive dominance wasn't surprising. In their previous seven games at Gillette Stadium, the Patriots had given up just three touchdowns. So no one in Reliant Stadium was surprised when, late in the second quarter of Super Bowl XXXVIII, the game was still scoreless. The Panthers had minus-7 yards total offense. Carolina quarterback Jake Delhomme was 1-for-9, passing for exactly one yard.

The Patriots should have had the lead, but sure-footed kicker Adam Vinatieri—who two years earlier had made a couple of clutch field goals in the snow in Foxboro to beat Oakland in overtime and then hit the last-second, game-winning field goal that beat the Rams in Super Bowl XXXVI in New Orleans—not only missed a 31-yarder but also had a 36-yard attempt blocked.

Those missed opportunities loomed large as the clock wound down toward halftime. Then all hell broke loose. After both teams had struggled to move the ball for the first 25 minutes, the game suddenly turned into a track meet, with the offenses zipping up and down the field. There were 61 points scored in the last 33:05—32 of them by the Patriots, 29 by the Panthers.

"What a game!" Brady said. "Fitting for the Super Bowl, I guess."

Brady had the Patriots on top 14–10 at halftime, thanks to a pair of five-yard touchdown passes to Deion Branch and David Givens. Those 24 points were scored in the last 3:05 of the first half. After a scoreless third quarter, the Pats and Panthers combined for 37 points in the final 15 minutes.

The Patriots made it 21–10 on a two-yard run by Antowain Smith 11 seconds into the fourth quarter. Carolina closed to 21–16 on a 33-yard run by DeShaun Foster, after which the Panthers tried a two-point conversion but didn't get it.

It looked as if the Pats were going to get at least three of those points right back until Brady, making an uncharacteristic mistake, was intercepted in the end zone with 7:38 remaining.

Three plays later Delhomme found Muhsin Muhammad behind the New England secondary and lofted a long bomb that Muhammad turned into an 85-yard touchdown—the longest play from scrimmage in Super Bowl history.

The Patriots, who had been on the brink of leading by at least eight points and quite possibly 12, suddenly found themselves behind 22–21 as the Panthers again tried for two and again failed to convert.

Wide receiver David Givens catches a touchdown pass from quarterback Tom Brady during the second quarter of Super Bowl XXXVIII in Houston on February 1, 2004. Photo courtesy of AP Images.

But the Pats had no need to worry. They had Brady, who efficiently moved the offense to the Carolina 1, where, on second down, he surprised the Panthers by throwing a touchdown pass to Mike Vrabel, a linebacker who often plays tight end in goal-line situations. It capped a big night for Vrabel, who, late in the second quarter, had caused the fumble by Delhomme that led to New England's first touchdown.

This time it was the Patriots' turn to try a two-point conversion. Unlike the Panthers, they made it—Kevin Faulk taking a direct snap from center and darting into the end zone for a 29–22 lead. It didn't last long, as Delhomme capped a seven-play, 80-yard, game-tying touchdown drive with a 12-yard pass to Ricky Proehl. Oddly it had been

Proehl who, playing for St. Louis two years earlier, caught a touchdown pass from Kurt Warner that tied Super Bowl XXXVI at 17–17 with 1:30 to play. That was enough time for Brady to get New England close enough for Vinatieri to kick the game-winning 48-yard field goal. This time, Brady had only 1:08 to work with.

He got a break when the Panthers' John Kasay booted his kickoff out of bounds, enabling New England to start at its 40-yard line.

"It was like déjà vu—a nightmare all over again," said Proehl. "You give Tom Brady the ball with a little over a minute and all he needs is 25 yards—it's tough."

No quarterback in the game today is mentally tougher or physically better in that situation than Brady. "Tom's tough in those situations at the end of a game," Belichick said. "He's accurate, he makes great decisions with the ball, and he has a lot of poise."

With 14 seconds left to play, the Patriots were in a third-and-3 situation at the Carolina 40—still too far away for a field goal. But Brady found Branch open down the right sideline for 17 yards, giving Vinatieri a chance to win the game.

Despite his problems in the first half, Vinatieri was perfect this time, from 41 yards, and the Patriots were champions again.

Brady won his second MVP trophy, setting a Super Bowl record by completing 32 passes (in 48 attempts) for a season-high 354 yards and three touchdowns, with one interception.

"Tom is a winner," Belichick said. "That's what a quarterback's job is—to do what he needs to do to make the team win. Tom does that as well as anybody."

Snowmen

You've heard of the Abominable Snowman? Well, the Patriots are the Invincible Snowmen. When the snow falls in Foxboro, so does the opposition. The Patriots are very much at home in the snow—a perfect 10–0 in Foxboro, including three playoff victories. To paraphrase the popular old song: "When the weather outside is frightful, the Pats are so delightful." Instead of dreading the snow, the Patriots delight in it.

"I love playing in bad-weather games," said linebacker Tedy Bruschi, who grew up in San Francisco and went to college at Arizona.

One of Bruschi's most memorable games occurred in the snow on December 7, 2003, against the Dolphins. The day before, a blizzard had dumped more than two feet of the white stuff across New England, making it difficult for fans to get to Foxboro. When those who were able to make the trip and find one of the limited parking spots finally got to their seats, they found them covered in snow. The stadium crew couldn't shovel them off because there was no place to put the snow that was removed. If they took it from one row, it would be tossed into another.

With a stiff wind blowing, both teams had difficulty moving the ball. The Patriots were protecting a slim 3–0 lead when Bruschi clinched the victory with a five–yard interception return for a touchdown late in the fourth quarter. As he knelt in the end zone, jubilant Pats fans celebrated with a spontaneously choreographed display of wintry pyrotechnics.

As the pounding sounds of Gary Glitter's "Rock and Roll, Part Two" were blasted over the stadium's speaker system, fans tossed handfuls of snow into the air in rhythm to the beat: "Bah-dum, bah-dah-dum, hey! (toss snow); bah-dum, bah-dah-dum, hey (toss snow).

It was a lovely sight to see. And a lot of fun, too.

"Seeing that snow flying got me in the holiday spirit," Bruschi said. "It made me want to go home and sit in front of the fire by my Christmas tree."

Patriots players have been known to celebrate spontaneously in the snow. When the Patriots rallied to beat the Raiders in the infamous "Tuck Rule" game in the 2001 AFC divisional playoffs on two field goals by Vinatieri, deep-snapper Lonie Paxton flung himself on his back in the end zone and moved his arms and legs back-and-forth, making snow angels. Which certainly was understandable, following what seemed a heaven-sent victory. Wide receiver Wes Welker made like the littlest angel when he celebrated in similar fashion after scoring a touchdown in the Patriots' 47–7 rout of the soon-to-be NFC champion Arizona Cardinals the Sunday before Christmas 2008.

Strangely, one of the Patriots' best "snowmen" was fullback Mosi Tatupu, a native Pacific Islander who was born in Pago Pago, American Samoa, grew up in Hawaii, and played his college ball at Southern Cal. But he seemed to be an Eskimo the way he ran through the snow in Foxboro.

Tatupu earned the sobriquet of the "Snowin' Samoan"—a variation on the nickname of quarterback Jack Thompson, who was known as the "Throwin' Samoan"—after rushing for a career-high 128 yards on 21 carries in a 7–0 win over the New Orleans Saints in early December 1983.

Described by center Pete Brock as resembling "a bowling ball with legs," the six-foot, 227-pound Tatupu scattered the Saints' tacklers like tenpins.

"I just read the holes, try to keep my balance, and stay as low as possible," Tatupu said. "You can't make quick cuts when the footing isn't good. You take what you can get. I just try to power forward and get the yards."

Tatupu had shown his ability to plow through the snow for yardage the year before in the famous Snow Plow game. While Patriots fans remember Henderson veering his John Deere tractor off the yard line to scrape a spot for Smith, what's often forgotten is that Tatupu gained 54 yards in the late drive that led to the field goal.

Teams hate to play the Patriots when it's snowing in New England because, invariably, they find themselves "snowed under."

Certainly, the Colts, who play in the climate-controlled comfort of a domed stadium in Indianapolis, weren't thrilled to have snow fall during successive playoff games in Foxboro against the Patriots, who beat them 24–14 in the 2003 AFC Championship Game and 20–3 in the conference semifinals the following season.

When Colts quarterback Peyton Manning looked up at the heavens, he had to realize he didn't have a prayer of beating the Patriots. When, as if on cue, the snow started coming down and coming down hard, the Patriots and their fans knew the Colts would be going down and going down hard.

chapter 15

Super Bowl XXXIX

Once again the Patriots came into the Super Bowl on a roll. The defending NFL champions were 16–2 overall. They had won 10 of their last 11 games and an amazing 31 of their last 33, dating back to the first Sunday of October 2003.

They had just beaten Indianapolis, the NFL's highest-scoring team (averaging more than 32 points a game) in the conference semifinals in Foxboro, holding Peyton Manning and the Colts to only a field goal in a 20–3 victory. In the AFC Championship Game in Pittsburgh against the 16–1 Steelers, who had given up fewer points than any team in the league (an average of just under 16 a game), the Patriots lit up the scoreboard, winning 41–27.

Still, veteran safety Rodney Harrison, one of the team's leaders, insisted that, no matter what the oddsmakers in Las Vegas said, the Patriots were underdogs against the Philadelphia Eagles in Super Bowl XXXIX.

"Everyone had pretty much blown us off, didn't give us a chance," he said, after the Patriots won their second straight title and third in four years by beating the Eagles 24–21. "Everyone picked Philly to win."

Everyone? How about hardly anyone? The Patriots were favored by seven in Vegas. In a poll of sportswriters from around the country who were in Jacksonville to cover the Super Bowl, 32 of 33 picked the Patriots to win. That didn't matter to Harrison and the Pats, who, in their own minds, convinced themselves they were the underdogs.

"We loved playing up that underdog role as much as possible," offensive coordinator Charlie Weis acknowledged later. "We always

Rodney Harrison (No. 37) intercepts a pass intended for the Philadelphia Eagles' Brian Westbrook (No. 36) as Patriots linebacker Tedy Bruschi (No. 54) helps on the play in the first quarter of Super Bowl XXXIX at Alltel Stadium on February 6, 2005, in Jacksonville, Florida. Photo courtesy of AP Images.

played the 'No one believes we can win' and 'It's us against the world' cards for everything they were worth."

It would seem they were worth quite a bit within the confines of the Patriots locker room. Outside it, however, they were worthless. Because the truth, at least in New England, was that almost no one believed the Patriots could lose, since they hardly ever did.

They had, however, lost 34–20 at Pittsburgh on Halloween, a defeat that snapped what had been a 21-game winning streak. Combined with the fact that the Steelers had won 15 in a row heading into the AFC Championship Game, there were plenty of people in Pittsburgh—and more than a few others around the country—who figured the Patriots' reign was about to come to an end. But it was the Steelers who came to grief and Harrison who blew the game open.

Less than two minutes after the opening kickoff, Eugene Wilson made the first of what would turn out to be three New England interceptions of Pittsburgh's rookie quarterback Ben Roethlisberger. The Pats turned that early turnover into a field goal.

Tom Brady then sandwiched a pair of touchdown passes—a 60-yarder to Deion Branch and a nine-yarder to David Givens (set up by a 45-yard completion to Branch)—around a Pittsburgh field goal to give New England a 17–3 advantage.

The touchdown bomb to Branch came immediately after the Patriots had stuffed Jerome "the Bus" Bettis on fourth-and-1 at the New England 39. That was a statement stop, declaring emphatically and dramatically that the Patriots were every bit as tough and physical as the Steelers. When Brady unloaded deep to Branch, it showed the Pats were faster and smarter, too.

While studying video of the Steelers defense, the Patriots had picked up the tendency of safety Troy Polamalu to line up over the slot receiver in situations where the offense used two tight ends and two wide receivers. The Pats felt they could use that to get Branch one-on-one with a cornerback, which is exactly what happened on the long touchdown pass when Polamalu wound up helping to double-cover David Givens crossing over the middle.

But what really put New England in control of the game was Harrison's interception and 87-yard return for a touchdown late in the first half, enabling the Patriots to take a 24–3 lead into the locker room.

"Rodney undercut the tight end on the 'out' route," Belichick said. "That was at least a 10-point swing—maybe more."

That interception was one of four Harrison had in the playoffs. He picked off two passes in the Super Bowl against the Eagles, including the one that sealed the victory in the final seconds.

"Rodney understands the game," linebacker Roman Phifer said. "He's a student of the game. He's played it for a long time, and he's able to tell you to look out for this on this play, look out for that on that play. It's a great testament to him.

"He's able to just go out there and play well, regardless of who is next to him. He's like, 'Yeah, put him in there, and then we're going to get it done.'"

What the Patriots did in St. Louis the first Sunday in November showed that, once again—despite what, to a team less physically talented and mentally tough, could have been a devastating rash of injuries—they were a championship-caliber club.

The Patriots went into that game against the air-oriented Rams offense without either of their starting cornerbacks, All-Pro Ty Law and Tyrone Poole. Then on the second play Asante Samuel was forced to the sideline when he hurt his shoulder bouncing 288-pound tight end Brandon Manumaleuna out of bounds.

For the remainder of the game, when the Patriots used six defensive backs in their "dime" coverage on passing downs, here's who was on the field: Harrison; starting free safety Eugene Wilson, in only his second NFL season; rookie Dexter Reid, a fourth-round draft choice; another rookie, Randall Gay, who was undrafted; Earthwind Moreland, brought up from the practice squad only the day before; and Troy Brown. That's right, Troy Brown, the veteran wide receiver and return specialist.

"I'm a football player," said Brown, as if filling in on defense after 12 years of playing offense was the most natural thing in the world. "I just want to play football. Any chance I have, I want to be out there. I just like playing ball."

Brown is a guy who should have played in the era of leather helmets without a face mask, back in the days of limited substitution, when players went both ways, playing both offense and defense.

He had been a star at Marshall in the early 1990s. As a senior in 1992 he caught 101 passes for 1,654 yards and 16 touchdowns. He also ran for two touchdowns. But it was as a return man that he was most dangerous, tying an NCAA single-season record by returning four kick-offs for touchdowns and setting a record by averaging 29.69 yards on 32 kickoff returns for his career.

Those numbers didn't impress the NFL scouts, however. It wasn't until the eighth—and final—round in 1993 that the Patriots drafted him with the 198th overall pick. He made the team as a rookie but was used mostly to return punts and kickoffs. The following year he was cut at the end of training camp by Bill Parcells. The Patriots re-signed him midway through that 1994 season, but Brown didn't make his first NFL start until 1997, when he filled in for the injured Terry Glenn.

It wasn't until Bill Belichick came to New England that Brown was truly given a chance to show what he could do. Made a full-time starter for the first time in 2000, he caught 83 passes that season and followed that up with what was then a team-record 101 in 2001, when the Patriots won their first Super Bowl. He also returned two punts for touchdowns that season and added a third in the postseason, when his 55-yard return provided the Pats with their first touchdown in the AFC Championship Game in Pittsburgh.

"He's the ultimate football player," said Brady, who was not just Brown's quarterback, but also one of his biggest fans.

That point was proven once again in the game in St. Louis in 2004, when, in addition to filling in capably on defense, Brown also caught three passes for 30 yards and a touchdown. That touchdown pass, by the way, wasn't from Brady. It was from kicker Adam Vinatieri.

Vinatieri had kicked four field goals in the first half and was lining up for what everyone inside the domed stadium assumed would be a chip-shot fifth, with the ball at the Rams' 4-yard line. No one noticed Brown loitering uncovered near the sideline.

"We hoped to catch them sleeping, and we did," Vinatieri said. "It's one of those things that you put in, and it just has to come up at the right time, the right opportunity. Troy kind of hid on the outside, and we snapped the ball before they noticed. I just threw it out there. I knew if I got it anywhere close to Troy, he'd catch it."

"We couldn't snap the ball fast enough to suit me," Brown said.

That wasn't the only unusual touchdown pass thrown that day. Earlier in the game linebacker Mike Vrabel, coming in to play tight end near the goal line, made a scoring grab that any receiver would have taken pride in, stretching out to catch the ball, then tapping the toes of both feet in the end zone before falling out of bounds.

"Today was a total team effort," said running back Corey Dillon, who rushed for 112 yards and a touchdown on 25 carries. "People were doing things they're unaccustomed to doing. They came through in the clutch. That's the mark of a good team—a true team."

"It was," Belichick said proudly, "as complete a team victory as I've ever been around. There were so many guys who stepped up. The Rams throw the ball very well. They have a great receiving group. But Earthwind and Gay and Troy went out there and battled. That's what this team is all about—being prepared to step up when called upon."

Belichick already had two teams that won Super Bowls. After that midseason game in St. Louis, he felt like the 2004 Patriots could win a third. Even with their top three corners out of action, the Pats had held one of the league's most wide-open offenses to just two touchdowns. They showed heart and character, ingenuity and creativity, adaptability and resiliency.

Brown embodied all of those traits.

"I couldn't play wide receiver," Harrison said. "For Troy to make plays on offense, then come back in and play the slot receiver man-to-man—that shows how versatile he is."

The Patriots as a team were versatile. And talented. And tenacious. And unselfish. And extremely well coached by Belichick and his staff, which featured coordinators Charlie Weis (offense)—who would leave after that season to become head coach at Notre Dame—and Romeo Crennel (defense) who also left, to become coach of the Cleveland Browns.

By beating the Eagles, the Patriots became only the second team (joining the Dallas Cowboys) to win three Super Bowls in four seasons.

"Someday," veteran linebacker Willie McGinest said, "I'm going to have kids and tell them I played on one of the greatest teams of all time." It's hard to imagine anyone disputing that.

The Patriots do not merely pay lip-service to the concept of playing as a team, of being unselfish, of knowing one's role and playing it to the best of one's ability.

"Everybody buys into the team concept," linebacker Matt Chatham said. "We'd be stupid not to."

Brady had been the MVP of New England's first two Super Bowl victories, but this time the award went to Branch, who had 11 receptions for 133 yards. It was his second straight spectacular Super Bowl. He'd caught 10 passes for 143 yards and a touchdown in the Patriots' 32–29 win over Carolina the year before, which is partly the reason Brady was so happy to see his favorite target get the recognition he deserved.

"It's awesome to see Deion win it," said Brady, as happy as if he won the award himself. "He's done everything he can for this team. This is a team full of guys who cheer for one another. The MVP is nice, but that's not why you play. I'm playing for that diamond ring that's big as a belt buckle."

The New England defense earned its rings by intercepting McNabb three times and sacking him four times. Linebacker Mike Vrabel, reprising his role as tight end he plays so well, caught a touchdown pass, just as he had in St. Louis and in Super Bowl XXXVIII against the Panthers.

"When you work together," linebacker Tedy Bruschi said, "when you embrace words like *dignity*, *integrity*, and *unselfishness*, great things can be accomplished."

By winning their third Super Bowl in four years, the Patriots established their credentials as one of the NFL's all-time great teams—something that anyone who had seen that midseason game in St. Louis had known for a while.

Tedy

It couldn't have been more sudden, more startling, or more frightening. Just three days after playing in his first Pro Bowl, only 10 days after winning his third Super Bowl championship ring, Tedy Bruschi suffered a stroke he feared would end his football career at the age of 31.

He'd only just come back from Hawaii when, in the early morning hours of February 15, 2005, he was stricken. Taken in an ambulance to Massachusetts General Hospital in Boston, he underwent extensive tests, one of which revealed that, in addition to having had a stroke, he also had a hole in his heart that would need to be closed.

Three days later Bruschi was able to walk out of the hospital with his wife, Heidi, holding his hand. But his vision was limited, he was walking robotically, and his primary concern was not whether he'd be able to play football again, but whether he'd ever be able to play again with his three young sons—all under the age of five—including baby Dante, who was only one month old.

At first he didn't think he would play again. Certainly, Heidi did not want him to play again. She was understandably worried about what could happen to her husband if he tried to return to football.

That didn't seem possible early on, and Bruschi told team owner Robert Kraft and coach Bill Belichick that his playing days were over. They assured him he could have a job in the organization if he wanted one.

But as his rehab progressed during the spring and early summer, Bruschi felt more and more as if he might be able to come back. He began to consider sitting out the 2005 season and returning to the Patriots in 2006.

Heidi didn't want to hear it. She was vehemently opposed to the idea of her husband, who turned 32 that June, returning to the violent world of profession football.

But he received medical clearance and, during the summer, began to gear his workouts toward getting into football shape.

He didn't go to training camp, instead working out on his own with Mike Woicik, the team's strength and conditioning coach. Meanwhile the Patriots placed him on the Physically Unable to Perform (PUP) list, which meant he could be activated after the sixth game of the season.

Heidi was hardly the only one who had her doubts. Former players Tom Jackson, Steve Young, and Michael Irvin all said on ESPN that Bruschi should retire. But he was progressing well, he was happy, and Heidi—finally convinced by the doctors that her husband was healthy again—said she would support him, knowing how much he loved the game, how much it was a part of him.

On October 19 Bruschi returned to practice with his teammates, preparing for a nationally televised Sunday-night game in Gillette Stadium against Buffalo on October 30.

When he was introduced to the excited crowd—Bruschi always had been one of the most popular Patriots because of the combination of his ability and infectious enthusiasm—he heard what he called "the loudest ovation of my career. It still gives me chills when I think about it."

It wasn't merely a token appearance. Bruschi was on the field for 76 plays that night, including playing on special teams, and made 10 tackles as the Patriots won 21–16. It was a performance that earned him AFC Defensive Player of the Week honors.

"I played all right," he said. "I was rusty and winded. I could feel my legs weakening in the third quarter. I think the award was the NFL's way of acknowledging everything I'd been through."

In order to encourage other stroke victims, Bruschi wrote a book about his experiences, titled *Never Give Up*.

"I know this might sound crazy to some people," he wrote, "given the consequences involved, but I had to try. I didn't want to be mentally punishing myself five or 10 years [later] by saying, 'You didn't even try.' Of course, the other side of the argument is that trying—especially if something goes wrong—might prevent me from being the same in five years. Or prevent me from being around at all.

"I don't believe that life should be lived through a series of what-ifs. You have to be smart and cautious, but after you've educated yourself on whatever it is that you fear, you can't live a timid life, afraid of what might be hiding around the corner. You have to show courage."

Bruschi showed he was as good as ever, despite having had a stroke. He started nine games the remainder of the 2005 season, then led the team in tackles in 2006 and 2007.

Tom Brady, in the foreword to Bruschi's book, described how the veteran linebacker's teammates feel about him. "Tedy gives you something to believe in," he wrote. "Whether we're winning or losing, he holds his head high, and he knows himself and handles himself so well, others can't help but follow him. The way he practices and plays forces you to become a better teammate; the way he demands hustle and toughness forces you to become a better leader; and the way he carries himself inspires you to become a better person.

"This made his return to playing all the more electrifying," Brady continued. "The stadium was louder that night than the nights we had raised our Super Bowl banners. Our captain, our leader, our inspiration was back on the field doing what he loved to do."

chapter 16

Almost Perfect

The Patriots were *this close*—2:39 away—from a perfect season in 2007. They were *this close*—83 yards to stop the New York Giants—from a 19–0 record and their fourth NFL championship in seven years. But they couldn't close the deal.

When the Patriots lost Super Bowl XLII to the Giants, they lost more than a game. They lost a prominent place in NFL history.

"We've always said you're defined in this league by championships and not how many regular-season games you can win," linebacker Mike Vrabel said. "People always remember the champion."

The Patriots were going to be remembered as the best team of all time, winners of 19 consecutive games, surpassing the 1972 Miami Dolphins, who went 17–0 and beat the Redskins in Super Bowl VII. It was going to be more than merely a Super Sunday for the undefeated Pats. It was going to be a Superb Sunday, a perfect ending to a perfect season

"This game is about history," linebacker Junior Seau said during the week leading up to Super Bowl XLII. "It's the chance of a lifetime, something to look back on and be very proud of for years to come."

But the Patriots missed that once-in-a-lifetime chance. They had football immortality in their hands and let it slip through their fingers—literally.

"It's the biggest game of all our lives—my life, the entire team, our coaches," said quarterback Tom Brady, who has a history of coming up big in the biggest games.

"We're going to be remembering this game," Brady said, "for as long as we live, win or lose."

He was right about that. Unfortunately Super Bowl XLII turned out to be a game that Patriots fans would rather forget. What was supposed to be a coronation ended in devastation, near-ecstasy becoming abject agony, elation turning to anguish.

"We just didn't get the ball into the end zone enough. That got us beat," Brady said after the Patriots lost 17–14.

They didn't get the ball into the end zone enough. Did anyone who watched the New England offense throughout its spectacular, record-setting 2007 season ever think they'd hear those words? Did any Pats fan who watched Brady and company make the scoreboard light up like a pinball machine think it would be a lack of offense that would get the Patriots beat?

The Pats had scored more points—589—than any team in NFL history. They averaged 37 points a game. They scored 31 or more points in 12 of their 16 games and scored at least 20 in every game. In the final game of the regular season, against the Giants at the Meadowlands, they'd won a 38–35 shootout.

They'd beaten the Cowboys in Dallas 48–27 when both teams were 5–0. Then they went to Miami and trounced the Dolphins 49–28, after which they routed the Redskins 52–7. At the midpoint of the season the Patriots' smallest margin of victory was 17 points (34–17 over Cleveland).

On November 4 the Patriots played at Indianapolis, marking the latest date in an NFL season that two undefeated teams had met. The Patriots came out on top 24–20, enjoyed their "bye" week, then went to Buffalo and put up a season-high 56 points in a 56–10 blasting of the Bills. They cooled off a bit after that, barely slipping past the Eagles 31–28, and they were lucky to win 27–24 the next weekend at Baltimore. But there was no stopping them in their pursuit of perfection.

By the end of the regular season, Brady had passed for an NFL-record 50 touchdowns. Randy Moss had caught 23 of them, also an NFL record. Wes Welker had 112 receptions, a franchise record.

To the surprise of no one, the Patriots won both conference playoff games at home, disposing of Jacksonville 31–20, then beating San Diego for the second time—the Pats knocked them off 38–14 in Foxboro the second week of the season—this time by a score of 21–12.

That set up a rematch with the Giants, whose fearsome pass rush certainly was a cause for concern. But hadn't the Patriots handled it just a month earlier and done so with two starters out?

Brady had thrown 578 passes during the regular season and was sacked just 21 times. Three of his offensive linemen—left tackle Matt Light, left guard Logan Mankins, and center Dan Koppen—were voted to the Pro Bowl.

But the Giants sacked Brady five times. Light couldn't handle Osi Umenyiora. The Patriots had trouble finding Justin Tuck, who kept changing position along the Giants' defensive front. And even when they did manage to locate him, they couldn't block him.

Still, when the Patriots absolutely had to move the ball, when they needed to score or concede defeat, they did put up seven points. With Brady completing eight of 11 passes—the last a six-yard touchdown toss to Moss—New England drove 80 yards and took a 14–10 lead with 2:42 to go.

When rookie Ray Ventrone—signed, cut, and then re-signed several times from the practice squad during the season—raced downfield on the kickoff and nailed Domenik Hixon at the New York 17, the only question seemed to be which New England defender would make the play that would clinch the perfect season? The answer turned out to be no one. "We had our opportunities," Rodney Harrison said.

Yes, they certainly did. On second-and-5 at his own 44, with 1:20 remaining, New York quarterback Eli Manning threw toward David Tyree near the right sideline. The ball sailed a bit, and Patriots cornerback Asante Samuel went up to get it. He could have come down with it. He should have come down with it. But he didn't. Instead, he came up empty.

The next play was, in the words of Giants coach Tom Coughlin, "one of the great plays of all time in the Super Bowl."

With the pocket collapsing around him, it looked as if Manning was going to be sacked by defensive lineman Jarvis Green. Somehow Manning slipped out of Green's grasp, away from the scrum of defenders around him, and heaved the ball downfield, once again toward Tyree.

Harrison was covering Tyree, and the two of them jumped for the ball. Tyree went high enough to pin it against the top of his helmet, but as he fell to the ground there seemed no way he could hang on—especially with Harrison hanging all over him. Somehow, some way he did, for a gain of 32 yards.

Four plays later, with Ellis Hobbs in single coverage on Plaxico Burress at the New England 13, Manning threw a fade that Burress, who had faked Hobbs into heading in the opposite direction, caught for the winning touchdown with 35 seconds on the clock.

Defense wins championships? Not any more, apparently. Not in New England, anyway.

"The offense," said Patriots defensive end Richard Seymour, "put us in a great position to win. Defensively, we didn't get it done."

He paused, then uttered what would be the epitaph for the Patriots' bid to make history, their quest for a perfect season. "Our goal," Seymour said, "wasn't to be perfect. Our goal was to win the Super Bowl."

Moss and Welker

Randy Moss is everything you'd want in a wide receiver.

He's tall and strong at 6'4" and 210 sinewy pounds. He's also fast, with a 4.4 speed in the 40. He's a marvelous athlete, possessing long arms, huge hands, and outstanding leaping ability that helped him twice win Player of the Year honors as a high school basketball player in West Virginia.

Wes Welker is short—5'9" on tiptoes. He's listed at 185 pounds but looks lighter. He's quick rather than flat-out fast. All of these reasons represent why hardly anybody wanted him as a wide receiver coming out of high school, even though he'd been Player of the Year in Oklahoma, and why, even though he set NCAA records as a punt returner at Texas Tech, he wasn't drafted by the NFL.

Together now in New England, the two of them are as dangerous a pair of wideouts as there is in the AFC. They complement each other perfectly. While Moss is scary, Welker is pesty. While Moss is frightening, Welker is frustrating. While Moss' specialty is touchdowns, Welker's is first downs.

"He's a mismatch every time he's out there," quarterback Tom Brady says of Moss, who came to New England from Oakland in 2007 for what

Patriots receiver Randy Moss (No. 81) picks up yardage after a reception against the New York Giants in the fourth quarter of Super Bowl XLII at University of Phoenix Stadium on February 3, 2008, in Glendale, Arizona. Photo courtesy of AP Images.

now seems the ridiculously low, bargain-basement price of a fourth-round draft choice.

He had been unhappy in Oakland, where the Raiders won just six games in his two years there, and the Raiders were disappointed in him, feeling he didn't give his best all the time. In New England Moss has been, as the song goes, "simply the best—better than all the rest."

Brady, after years of making do with what might charitably be described as an average bunch of receivers plus Deion Branch, felt like a kid at Christmas when Moss and Welker—obtained from Miami for a second-round draft choice—were added to the roster.

Delighted with his new "toys," Brady threw for an NFL-record 50 touchdowns in 2007, as the Patriots went undefeated in the regular season, with 23 of those touchdown tosses—also a league record—going to Moss.

It is, as Brady points out, all but impossible to find anyone to match up with Moss one-on-one. He is equally capable of running past a defender, of outjumping a defender, or, if necessary, of outmuscling a defender for the football.

He was insulted in 2008 in Miami when the Dolphins elected to use single coverage against him most of the game. "I think they disrespected me by playing single coverage," Moss said. You'd think the Dolphins would have shown Moss more respect, considering he'd burned them for four touchdowns—two in each game—in 2007.

"I don't know why coach [Tony Sparano] disrespected me like that," said Moss. You can bet Sparano won't do it again. Not after Moss made eight receptions for 125 yards and three touchdowns as the Patriots demolished the Dolphins 48–28.

"I am who I am, and I love to do what I do," Moss said. "If I see single coverage, I think I can beat anybody in this league, I don't care who it is. Anytime I feel disrespected, I want to go out there and make it happen."

Matt Cassel, who moved into the lineup when Brady was injured in the season opener in 2008, had marveled from the sideline at what Moss had done the year before. When he started throwing to him in games, he was even more impressed.

"I'm always amazed by what Randy can do," Cassel said. "He's got amazing hands and body control. He's able to control the defender with his body and then go up and get the ball. He's a special player."

In some ways, Welker is even more amazing. He's like a Timex watch—he takes a beating but keeps on ticking. He's like the Energizer bunny. He just keeps going, and going, and going. He's like those old, Joe Palooka, blow-up "bop bags" that, when you knock 'em down, they pop right back up.

In that same game in Miami where Moss was running wild, Welker took a highlight-film hit from Channing Crowder, the Dolphins' 250-pound linebacker, that left him laying on the ground for a minute, looking as if he'd been hit by a locomotive, before he wobbled to the sideline.

Three plays later he was back in the game, catching a pass for a seven-yard gain. It was one of eight receptions he had, for 120 yards, including a career-high 64-yarder on which he tap-danced along the sideline, somehow managing to stay in bounds when it seemed he was about to go out.

"He's tough," coach Bill Belichick said. "Most of the time, he seems to manage to miss those solid blows. He gets them when they're kind of glancing, or he squirts under then. But every once in a while they tag him.

"But he tends to bounce right back. That's pretty impressive. He's smaller than I am, and you know those hits have got to hurt."

Welker downplayed it afterward. "I just had the breath knocked out of me," he said. "It's like when you get slapped around by your older brother. You get back up and come back with a pool stick."

Moss routinely makes special breathtaking plays—one-handed catches while running at full speed deep down the sideline, leaping grabs over defenders in the end zone. He's a game-breaker, a difference-maker.

Welker's specialty is making the routine plays, the ones that move the chains, that put the team in position to win games. And he makes a lot of them. After setting a franchise record for receptions in 2007 with 112 for 1,175 yards and eight touchdowns, he almost broke it in 2008, making 111 catches for 1,165 yards and three touchdowns. As if they weren't enough, he also has been the Pats' primary punt-returner the past two years and occasionally returns kickoffs as well.

As a slot receiver Welker is the guy who consistently gets open underneath when Moss stretches the secondary. Welker seldom drops a ball and has a knack for picking up yardage after the catch.

"He's been a very productive player for us," said Josh McDaniels, who in 2009 left his job as offensive coordinator in New England to become head coach of the Denver Broncos. "He's given us an element of catch-and-run yards that don't always get measured in practice. You throw a five-yard completion in practice, it looks like a five-yard completion. You throw that to him in a game, and it turns into a 25-yard gain. Wes has made a lot of plays for us."

It was because Welker had made so many plays against New England when he was playing for Miami that the Patriots decided they needed to get him.

"We couldn't handle him," Belichick said. "We played against him twice a year and we couldn't handle him—couldn't tackle him, couldn't cover him. He was a tough guy for us to match up with.

"He's a really competitive guy. He's tough, he's smart, he has good hands, good concentration, and he works hard. He does a lot of things well."

Moss can do a lot of things exceptionally well, but his work ethic had been questioned in Minnesota, despite some highly productive seasons for the Vikings. It was also called into question in Oakland, where he was said to take plays off—that he didn't always come off the line hard, that he loafed on routes when he wasn't likely to be getting the ball. The Patriots have seen none of that.

"I just wanted to come here and play some good football," Moss said. "That was my mind-set. What was special about breaking Jerry Rice's record [for touchdown receptions in a season] was shutting up all my critics, all those people who said negative things about me."

The Patriots have had nothing but good things to say about Moss. As for Welker, well, who doesn't love a guy who is like Rudy—the walk-on in the popular movie about Notre Dame who's "five-foot-nuthin'" and weighs "a hundred-and-nuthin'"—except he has talent. Big talent, even though he's a little guy. It's what he's always done, even though people always have wondered if he was big enough, if he was good enough.

"Pop Warner, middle school, high school, college, the pros—people always have questioned whether I could play," he said. "You've just got to believe in yourself."

At every level, Welker has made believers of his doubters. Texas Tech was the only big-time football school to offer him a scholarship, but Welker became a star for the Red Raiders. A three-time, All–Big 12 selection, he finished his college career with 259 receptions for 3,069 yards and 21 touchdowns and left Texas Tech as the all-time NCAA leader in punt-return yards (1,761) and touchdowns (eight).

Despite that, he still wasn't drafted by the NFL. Signed as a free agent by San Diego, the Chargers cut him in September 2004, his rookie year, after he'd returned four kickoffs in the season opener.

He quickly caught on with the Dolphins, who used him to return punts and kickoffs. The next year, he also started catching passes for Miami—29 in 2005, then 67 in 2006. He caught the eye of Belichick and Scott Pioli in New England, where his career has taken off.

"He has great quickness, great hands," Brady said. "He's so elusive, and he's fearless going over the middle."

"He's an all-around football player, a guy you can rely on," Cassel said. "I look to him constantly in pressure situations because I know he's going to get open. Everybody looks up to him, because he gives you 150 percent on every play."

"He's one of the most inspirational guys we've got," the Pats big left tackle, Matt Light, said of Welker. "He's as tough as they come."

He's also a true team player. "I'll do whatever they ask me to do," Welker said. "I just go out there and do my job each and every play to the best of my ability."

If he happens to get pounded in the process, well, that's just part of the game. "That's part of the job," he said. "You're going to take some vicious hits out there. You just have to make sure that you bounce back and get ready for the next play."

chapter 17

Dominant Dynasty

In the 1960s the Green Bay Packers were the Team of the Decade. The 1970s belonged to the Pittsburgh Steelers. The San Francisco 49ers were the team of the 1980s. In the 1990s it was the Dallas Cowboys, who for years had laid claim to being "America's Team." The New England Patriots can claim to be the Team of the 21st century.

Three championships. Four trips to the Super Bowl. Five AFC Championship Game appearances. A perfect 16–0 regular-season record in 2007. Not just one, but two winning streaks of 21 games. Eight straight winning seasons. Five straight AFC East titles, six in seven seasons. Fourteen wins in 17 postseason games. A 36–4 record from the last game of 2002 through the season opener of 2005, and a 25–2 mark from mid-December 2006 through mid-September 2008. No other team in this decade comes close to matching that record.

Dynasties, admittedly, aren't what they used to be back in the days when the Yankees dominated baseball, the Celtics hung championship banners from the rafters of the Boston Garden as often as a washer-woman hangs laundry, and the Stanley Cup seemed to have a permanent home in Montreal.

But in these days of the salary cap, parity scheduling, and the draft, the Patriots of this decade have been as dominant as any NFL team is likely to be for the foreseeable future.

Such things, however, are for Patriots fans to think about and debate. The players and coaches don't give them a second thought, nor do they like to talk about them.

"I'll leave the comparisons, the historical perspectives, to everybody else," coach Bill Belichick says.

Paul Tagliabue, who was commissioner of the NFL when the Patriots beat the Eagles in Super Bowl XXXIX, compared Belichick and the Pats to the name on the trophy he was presenting them: Vince Lombardi, the legendary coach of the Packers.

"You join the elite teams in the history of the National Football League," Tagliabue said. "Your ninth consecutive playoff victory ties the record of the Green Bay Packers. As I give you the trophy, I suspect coach Lombardi would have deep admiration for how your team played."

The Patriots would win a 10th straight postseason game the following year, before losing at Denver in the AFC semifinals.

They reached the conference championship game in 2006, losing to the Colts in Indianapolis when Peyton Manning led a late drive to pull out a 38–34 victory.

In 2007 New England went undefeated—a perfect 16–0—during the regular season, then beat Jacksonville and San Diego in the AFC playoffs before losing Super Bowl XLII to the New York Giants on a last-minute touchdown.

Although the Patriots didn't make the playoffs in 2008, they still finished 11–5, even though their star quarterback, Tom Brady, was lost for the season with a knee injury in the first quarter of the first game.

Matt Cassel, who hadn't started a game since high school, showed he could start for many teams in the league, passing for 21 touchdowns while throwing just 11 interceptions as the Patriots became only the second team to win 11 games and not qualify for postseason play since the NFL went to a 16-game schedule in 1978.

Clearly, the New England organization of this decade has been one to admire, establishing itself as a model franchise, one to be emulated throughout the league. But the Patriots don't play the comparison game, only football games.

"Dynasties," said former offensive coordinator Charlie Weis, now the head coach at Notre Dame, "are things that are talked about decades later. When you're living the experience, you don't think about it."

The last eight seasons, from 2001 to 2008, have been an enjoyable experience for just about everyone who's worn a New England uniform.

"We've never proclaimed ourselves anything," Tom Brady said. "That's not our style. We just have a lot of fun playing together.

"It's become a cliché with us, but we really are a team. I've never had a receiver complain about not getting the ball. I've never had a running back complain about not getting enough carries. I have an offensive line that busts their butts every game. And we have a defense that's just unnerving.

"For us, it's not so much about what we've accomplished in the grand scheme of things. You take one game at a time." It's an old cliché, and most players and coaches pay it only lip service, but the Patriots truly do take their seasons one game at a time. They don't look ahead. They never look back. They focus only on the game at hand.

During their lengthy winning streaks, the players always said things like, "We haven't won 12 in a row. We've won one in a row 12 times." It may be corny, but it works very, very effectively.

"We have a great group of guys," said Brady, "who are very selfless, just committed to winning. They're guys who work hard and listen to their coach, respect their coach. And when we get out on the field, we all have the same thing in mind. It's fun to lead a group of guys where there's no other agenda but winning games.

"I look at so many other teams and it's like they have 'personalities.' There's some people with good personalities and some who can distract from what you're doing. If you don't have everybody working in the same direction it becomes self-defeating. It's hard enough to win a game each week if you're doing everything the right way. Now when you have factors that are fighting against you, it's that much more difficult."

The Patriots have brought in players with "difficult" personalities. One was running back Corey Dillon, who came from Cincinnati. Another was wide receiver Randy Moss, who came from Oakland. It was generally acknowledged that, while talented, they could be trouble.

In New England, the only trouble they caused was for other teams. In 2004 Dillon was the punishing runner the Pats needed to improve their ground game and complement Brady's prolific passing. He racked up 1,635 yards and 12 touchdowns on 345 carries as the Patriots rolled to a second straight Super Bowl victory. He went on to lead the team in rushing again the next two years, gaining 733 yards and scoring 12 touchdowns in 2005 and picking up 812 yards while scoring 13 touchdowns in 2006.

All Moss did when he combined with Brady was catch an NFL season-record 23 touchdown passes and break Stanley Morgan's team record for receiving yards, gaining 1,493 on 98 catches, to Morgan's 1,491.

Eyebrows were raised when the Patriots signed those two players, but they fit in well in New England, adjusting quickly to what Belichick and Scott Pioli, who left after the 2008 season to take over the football operation in Kansas City, call the "Patriots Way."

"The Patriots Way," Pioli said, "is about a group of people who work passionately together and work very hard. It starts with hard work, discipline, and creating a culture where everyone is on the same page, everyone knows their role, everyone believes in the system, and everyone does their job. People understand their roles and they are selfless about their roles. That is the core of the 'Patriots Way.'

"Bill had the final say in everything," Pioli continued. "However, it was a collaboration. I'm not sure I can think of many players who ever came into the program that Bill and I didn't completely agree on. Because of the amount of respect that he and I had for one another, if there was a disagreement, the respect for the other person led us away from that player. It was one of the unique experiences that I've had— where Bill and I would agree on certain things, but when we'd disagree, we didn't have any issues. It was never a battle over ego. We were more honed in on coming up with the right answer rather than his answer or my answer. It was about the right answer. It was a true collaboration."

The veteran players quickly get the message across to newcomers. "Any person who thinks he's above anything or anyone is not going to last here," linebacker Tedy Bruschi said. "If there's a guy like that, we're going to let him know there's one way we do things around here—that's collectively, with hard work and preparation."

Rodney Harrison explained things more bluntly and amusingly when asked, in the summer of 2007, if he thought Moss might be reluctant to get with the Patriots' program. "If he doesn't," Harrison said, "I'll kick his butt. If he still doesn't get it, Bruschi will kick his butt. And, if he still doesn't get it, then Brady—well, Brady wouldn't be able to kick his butt, but he'd give him a good talking-to."

When football fans talk about the best teams of past decades, there shouldn't be any argument that the first decade of the 21st century belongs to the Patriots.

sources

Books

Bruschi, Tedy with Michael Holley. *Never Give Up*. Hoboken, NJ: John Wiley & Sons, 2007.

Donaldson, Jim. *Stadium Stories*. Guilford, CT: Insiders' Guide, 2005.

Fox, Larry. *The New England Patriots: Triumph and Tragedy*. New York: Atheneum, 1979.

Harris, David. *The League: The Rise and Decline of the NFL*. New York: Bantam Books, 1986.

Holley, Michael. *Patriots Reign*. New York: William Morrow, 2004.

McGuane, George. *The New England Patriots: A Pictorial History*. Virginia Beach, VA: Jordan & Co., 1980.

Pierce, Charles P. *Moving the Chains: Tom Brady and the Pursuit of Everything*. New York: Farrar, Straus and Giroux, 2006.

Weis, Charlie with Vic Carucci. *No Excuses*. New York: HarperEntertainment, 2006.

Newspapers and Magazines

Providence Journal

Sports Illustrated